The Job Crisis
for Black Youth

The Twentieth Century Fund Task Force on Employment Problems of Black Youth

The Praeger Special Studies program—utilizing the most modern and efficient book production techniques and a selective worldwide distribution network—makes available to the academic, government, and business communities significant, timely research in U.S. and international economic, social, and political development.

The Job Crisis for Black Youth

Report of the
Twentieth Century Fund
Task Force on Employment
Problems of Black Youth

With a Background Paper by
Sar A. Levitan and
Robert Taggart III

Praeger Publishers   New York   Washington   London

PRAEGER SPECIAL STUDIES IN U.S. ECONOMIC AND SOCIAL DEVELOPMENT

PRAEGER PUBLISHERS
111 Fourth Avenue, New York, N.Y. 10003, U.S.A.
5, Cromwell Place, London S.W.7, England

Published in the United States of America in 1971
by Praeger Publishers, Inc.

Library of Congress Catalog Card Number: 70-180869

Printed in the United States of America

A series of independent task forces made up of authorities with diverse experience and views has been created by the Twentieth Century Fund to deliberate over and to report on critical and urgent public issues. No issue has been more urgent or critical than unemployment of black youth, the topic of the dedicated group of experts whose findings appear on the following pages. In fact, the Fund's Task Force on Employment Problems of Black Youth regarded the situation as so serious that it made a public call for action before another hot summer set in. Its critical analysis and appeal, which received a good deal of attention in the communications media and by Congress, has already helped to bring about an expansion in the limited but useful programs for the young jobless in the nation's ghettos. But the report and the factual background paper that accompanies it make clear that much more needs to be done to keep unemployment from worsening among young black men and women and to lessen the threat of increased despair and hostility and violence.

The problem of forced idleness among black youth is far from new. Its roots lie deep in the nation's past. It has grown and festered over the years, partly because of the legacy of racism and the discrimination it produced and partly because of indifference and neglect. True, some significant steps have been taken, particularly after the explosion of a Watts or Newark or Washington, and yet the action of the past decade has been mostly too little and certainly too late. Perhaps the most acute symptoms have been treated and, for a time at least, checked. But the response has given rise to an unjustified sense of accomplishment and complacency. The ghetto is a no man's land for most Americans, who fail to recognize that the appalling lack of opportunity for black youth is a condition that continues to spread.

In sponsoring the Task Force on the unemployment of black youth, the Fund's Board of Trustees was evincing its concern about the failure to sustain a concerted and specific national effort to reduce the ranks of the jobless in the ghettos. But it did not—and could not—possess an accurate measure of the problem's extent or its increasingly heavy toll in economic waste and social disaffection. For black youth are the most victimized of the invisible poor whose plight was first publicized in Michael Harrington's *The Other America*, and there has been a paucity of reliable information on their numbers and lives. Even though opportunities have opened up for some, many know only the drudgery of dead end jobs or are condemned to the bleakness of a permanent place on the welfare rolls; others have no official existence except, of course, in the grim statistics of police dockets and city morgues.

The findings of the Task Force and the background paper dash the belief, once widely held, that achievement of full employment will benefit all Americans. The fact is that even when what passes for full employment is reached a substantial proportion of black youths are unable to find jobs. At a time like the present, when unemployment is well above the target, the rate of joblessness among young black men and women, especially the latter, soars to intolerable levels. And there is little expectation that general policies to stimulate the economy can do much, if anything, to cope with it. On the contrary, with more young blacks leaving the armed forces than entering, the prospect is that unemployment—and frustration and militancy—will climb still more.

Just as the problem is not new, the Task Force has acknowledged that there is no cheap or quick way to resolve it. The recommendations are constructive and realistic, involving both immediate action and long-term reform. Under the best of conditions, the Task Force believes, many more hot summers are unavoidable. And if a broad and concerted program embracing the government, private industry, trade unions, and educational facilities is not implemented, there is grave danger of an explosive crisis that will provoke radical actions and reactions.

While the Task Force is not optimistic, it is confident that there is still time to defuse the situation, provided the American people and their government are prepared to make firm commitments and live up to them. Now that the facts are known, it is the Task Force's hope that the public will recognize that it can no longer tolerate a state of affairs that makes a mockery of the nation's credo of equal rights and opportunities for all its citizens.

The Fund wants to express its appreciation to the Task Force on Employment Problems of Black Youth for the time and effort it gave to its analysis and recommendations. It also offers its thanks to Sar A. Levitan and Robert Taggart III of the Center for Manpower Policy Studies, The George Washington University, for their valuable background paper. The report and paper together provide, we believe, the most comprehensive review of the problem to date. All Americans should benefit from the result.

M. J. Rossant, *Director*
The Twentieth Century Fund

August, 1971

CONTENTS

List of Tables

List of Charts

REPORT
OF
THE
TASK FORCE

MEMBERS OF THE TASK FORCE

Eli Ginzberg, Chairman
Director
Conservation of Human Resources
Columbia University
New York, New York

Blanche Bernstein
Director of Research for
  Urban Social Problems
New School for Social Research
New York, New York

Eli Cohen
National Committee on
  Employment of Youth
New York, New York

Victor Gotbaum
American Federation of State,
  County and Municipal Employees
AFL-CIO District 37
New York, New York

Ernest Green
Director
Joint Apprenticeship Program
New York, New York

Sar A. Levitan
Center for Manpower Studies
The George Washington University
Washington, D.C.

Roy Providence
New York, New York

Robert Schrank
The Ford Foundation
New York, New York

Phyllis Wallace
Metropolitan Applied Research
  Center, Inc.
New York, New York

Seymour L. Wolfbein, Dean
School of Business Administration
Temple University
Philadelphia, Pennsylvania

I

When hope dies, its heirs are desperation and despair. A decade has passed since James B. Conant first warned of the "social dynamite" planted in our cities by the enforced idleness and empty expectation of "hundreds of thousands" of young people. By now, Conant's hundreds of thousands of the workless without hope have multiplied, while his warning has not yet been heeded.

The seeds of despair and desperation are apparent:

• At the height of this country's economic boom in 1969, more than 25 percent of nonwhite male and female teenagers in the central cities of our twenty largest metropolitan areas were unemployed. This constituted about 17 times the unemployment rate of 1.5 percent for white males in the entire country.

• Since 1969, the softening economy has led to a serious deterioration in the overall employment situation. But its effect on black youths has been a disaster. There are about 1.2 million black teenagers and 1.3 million blacks between the ages of twenty and twenty-four in metropolitan areas with populations of more than 250,000. As against a white adult unemployment rate of 4.6 percent during the second quarter of 1971, the overall black teenage unemployment rate was 34.9 percent—or more than 7 times greater; in the poverty areas it was 39.1 percent. For black adults between the ages of twenty and twenty-four, the unemployment rate was 19 percent.

• Even so, the official figures do not portray the extent of the problem. An additional number of the ghetto jobless are never found by the enumerators. At the very least, 100,000 young black people—a most conservative estimate—have given up hope and have stopped looking for jobs.

- A step above the dropouts from the labor market and the unemployed are those who have found jobs. But for many the step leads no higher. Their jobs provide fewer hours of work than those of whites, less pay, little permanence, and fewer prospects for advancement. Delayed, in some instances, but not in the end denied, they have not escaped the frustration of a dead-end work life.

- Compounding the hardships of slack in the job market and the handicap of race is the sex disadvantage with which black women must contend. They are held back by multiple layers of discrimination. The highest unemployment rates of any group are those for black female teenagers in low-income areas of central cities. Their unemployment rate in recent years has seldom been below 33 percent and is often as high as 50 percent.

- A growing minority of black youth now have the preparation to enter and complete junior or senior college or to acquire a manual or technical skill that can aid them in a job search. But they too continue to face major discrimination in the world of work, which takes its toll by forcing them to accept jobs at lower incomes, with less opportunity for advancement than the jobs for which they are qualified.

- While many black youths in urban ghettos are on tracks that do not lead into society's mainstream of legitimate gainful activity, their rural brothers in the farmlands and small towns of the South have even fewer employment prospects.

- After Conant's warning, two factors decelerated but did not negate the growth of unemployment among black youth. One was the economic expansion of 1961-69, the longest in our history, which generated an average of 1.5 million new jobs each year. The other was the expansion of the armed services, which drew more than a million additional young men, many black, out of the labor force. But the moderating influence of these factors no longer exists. Now, opposite trends are at work. Our economy is haltingly recovering from a recession, and the present national unemployment rate is over 6 percent, with little short-run prospect of dropping. This level further diminishes the opportunities for black youths whose hardships were crippling even while the boom was in full swing. Moreover, great numbers are pouring into the labor market from an accelerated demobilization of the armed forces while the draft draws fewer and fewer out, leading to intensified competition for the fewer jobs available.

• The urgent problem of race in a surplus and discriminatory labor market is daily growing more acute. More young black people will enter the job market in the decade ahead, and they will represent a higher proportion of all new entrants than they have in the past. Teenagers among blacks and other minority groups will increase from about 2.1 million in 1970 to 2.6 million in 1980—a gain of 24 percent. Among young adult blacks aged from twenty to twenty-four, the projections show an increase from under 2.2 million to about 3 million—a gain of 36 percent.

It is only at the gravest peril to our society that the American people continue to ignore the growing frustration, despair, and hostility that characterize, more and more, young black people. After a childhood and adolescence stunted by deprivation, rejection, and neglect, these young people want the opportunity to support themselves and to live useful lives. But, as the reports of the Equal Employment Opportunity Commission and other government agencies underscore, many desirable training and employment opportunities remain closed to black youth.

Many black young people have grown up in households with only one natural parent. They have lived in slum housing in slum neighborhoods where violence and crime are commonplace. They have attended schools where teachers do not teach them, where the curriculum is irrelevant, and where there are no performance standards. The family that should have nurtured them, the school that should have instructed them, the community that should have opened opportunities for them, the democratic society whose professed faith should have encouraged them—all have failed. They reach adulthood with one basic achievement not to be despised: they have survived their environment.

What they most need is a second chance to find themselves, to fit into a society that, through neglect—or worse—has seriously handicapped them. If there are walls they cannot scale that keep them out of jobs or confine them to the drudgery of ill-paid dead end work, then they are doomed to live permanently as marginal workers, to exist forever on welfare, to dwell in the twilight zone of illegal employment or to exist as criminals in and out of prison. A society that turns its back on them invites only the enmity of the young and puts its own future in grave jeopardy.

To be black in a society that is only slowly shedding its racist past is a handicap. To be poor in a society where the important developmental opportunities that parents provide for their children depend on money is a handicap. To be female in a society that continues to treat girls and women as inferiors is a handicap. As if the lack of social justice was not enough, the disequality creates a malignancy that puts at risk the established social order.

The American people have not been willing to respond to the Randolph-Rustin Freedom Budget of some years ago that called for investing $100 billion over ten years to rebuild the ghetto areas and to relocate the adults and children who were trapped in them. Instead, they have accepted a series of *ad hoc* measures, mere palliatives rather than basic solutions, and then only after trouble either erupts or threatens. For example, in June 1971, the federal government made a gesture acknowledging the approach of a hot summer. In early spring, the president requested a supplemental appropriation of $64.3 million for summer jobs for 514,000 young people. Congress, at the end of May, voted $105 million for 609,000 jobs. About 40 percent of the young people who got summer jobs under this program were black or other minority youth in low-income areas of our large cities. While these young people acquired a little work experience and a few may even have acquired modest skills on these summer jobs, most of them profited primarily from the approximately $375 that they earned if they worked the entire summer. This annual pattern of pseudo-resolution of the crisis is now well established.

The president, the Congress, and the American people hope that riots can be prevented with the provision of a modicum of summer jobs. But large numbers of black youths are left without jobs and income throughout the year, and the private sector is not able to come even close to meeting the needs of those who are not federally employed. So the dynamite remains primed for explosion.

II

The absence of desirable employment and career opportunities for large numbers of black youths is a failure that our society must correct without delay. There is urgent need for constructive action because of the widening gap between the expectations of black youth for full participation in American society and the realities of continued exclusion, deprivation, and discrimination. Over the longer term, the American people must address themselves with even greater seriousness to those defects in our institutions that have created and continue to enlarge the problem. An analysis of these defects and the Task Force's recommendations for their remedy are in the following sections of this report. Here, the Task Force strongly urges immediate, priority actions:

- The establishment of public service jobs for all young people who are unable to secure employment in the private sector.
- Adequate funding for antidiscrimination efforts in federal, state, and local governments to speed the removal of all arbitrary racial, ethnic, and sex barriers.
- The expansion of services, including child care and family planning, and of part-time employment opportunities for young black women who are currently out of school and out of work.

These actions are urgently required not only on grounds of justice and equity to the black community but also to ensure that our society does not become the target of those who see no alternative to violence to secure their rights.

III

Our social and economic institutions are defective in several ways:

- The national economy has consistently failed to generate a sufficient number of jobs at adequate wages for all who want to work. There remains a wide gap between the promise in the Employment Act of 1946 and its fulfillment.
- In allocating jobs, especially the better ones, our society has consistently discriminated against black people. More than a hundred years after the Thirteenth, Fourteenth, and Fifteenth Amendments to the Constitution, black people are still denied equal treatment in every facet of their lives—where they are permitted to live, the

schools they attend, the hospitals that treat them, their encounters with the police and the courts.

• The educational system permits a disturbingly large number of black and other minority young people to drop out or graduate from high school without the minimum skills they need to qualify for the wide range of desirable jobs.

• Our society lacks effective developmental institutions for adolescents who need an alternative to formal schooling.

• Our mechanisms to facilitate the transition of young people from school to work are ineffective.

• If alternative supplies of labor are available, employers are unwilling to hire young people or hire them primarily for dead end jobs that provide little training or that contribute little to the development of good work habits.

IV

To remedy these serious institutional defects, the Task Force makes the following policy recommendations:

A Realistic Program of Youth Conservation

1. On the basis of the nation's recent experience, we conclude that the establishment and maintenance of a continuing high level of employment is an essential precondition for sustained progress in improving the job and career opportunities of all youth, particularly black youth. But even if the country were willing to tolerate rapid price rises as the cost of a continuing high level of employment, such a policy still would not generate an adequate number of jobs for teenage and young adult workers, particularly those who belong to minority groups. Accordingly, we recommend that *Congress enact legislation creating a substantial number of public service jobs that, through an educational and training component, can lead to career advancement.* We also propose that, as the country gains experience with this new program, *public service employment be provided for all young people who seek full-time employment and cannot find jobs in the private sector.* An economy that generates a trillion dollars GNP has the

competence, if it can find the will, to create useful work for all who are forced to be idle.

2. To be black means to be the victim of discrimination. Young black people have seen their parents denied jobs, promotions, stability of employment, and access to fringe benefits for no other reason than the color of their skin. They, in turn, face discrimination with the same destructive consequences for themselves and their children unless and until society moves energetically to reduce and eliminate it. We therefore recommend a redoubling of efforts to eliminate discrimination in employment by the following actions: *Congress should grant the Equal Employment Opportunity Commission the right to issue cease-and-desist orders; Title VII of the Civil Rights Act of 1964 should be amended to remove the exemption of state and local government from the provision of the act; federal, state, and local legislative bodies should increase their funding to antidiscrimination agencies so that they are better able to carry out their missions; private and nonprofit employers should* devote more time and effort to ensuring that their organizations *adopt strong affirmative action programs and see to it that they are implemented by middle and first-line management.*

3. Large employers, public as well as private, must consider more than they have in the past the effect of locational decisions on employment opportunities for black workers. A decision to move from the central city to a suburb may have the same effect as hanging out a sign "no blacks wanted" if blacks have no ready access to the location. Where interurban transport is in place, it is essential that the responsible agencies *establish schedules to facilitate travel by city residents to suburbs*, and where it is lacking, explore the feasibility of establishing *special bus routes.*

The federal government, with the assistance of state governments and private sector enterprises, *must facilitate the building of more low-income and middle-income housing outside the central cities and assure that blacks and other minorities have access to it*. Such action is essential to ensure that minority group members are not cut off from many desirable job opportunities.

Because of our conviction that, if discrimination in employment against blacks could be eliminated, a large part of the adverse labor market experience of black youth would disappear, we want to call attention to further remedies: *The federal government can do much more than it has yet done through its Office of Federal Contract Compliance* to insist through the use of statistical guidelines and other objective measures that contractors *intensify their affirmative action programs* to open opportunities for black workers. The same holds for the *additional leverage that the federal government can exert through a stricter enforcement of its policy of nondiscrimination in its grant-in-aid programs*, which total over $30 billion annually. We do not want to convey the impression that no progress is being made by the federal government in eliminating discrimination in employment. But we agree with the imagery of Theodore M. Hesburgh, chairman of the U.S. Civil Rights Commission, and urge that the dinosaur be prodded so that it will open its eyes. In matters of law enforcement, and certainly national leadership, the federal government must be out in front or the country will not follow.

4. Many young black women are particularly victimized because, in addition to the handicaps of race and low income, they face sex discrimination in terms of the jobs available, wages paid, and opportunities for advancement. The highest unemployment rates of any group are those for black female teenagers in low-income areas of the central cities. But many young female adults suffer additional handicaps. One of every four black women aged from twenty to twenty-four is an unmarried mother, and in low-income areas of our large cities 33 percent of all who have been married do not live with a spouse. Since many young black women leave high school because of pregnancy, we recommend that *the educational authorities make special efforts to enable these young women to continue their studies during pregnancy and facilitate their return to school after the birth of their children*. Without a high school diploma, most of these young women will have no opportunity to prepare themselves for a desirable position in an increasingly white collar economy. To return to school or to obtain employment, these young women need ready access to child care facilities that are totally or substantially government subsidized. So we recommend that *federal, state, and local authorities, in cooperation with private and nonprofit organizations, assess the financial and other obstacles to a rapid expansion of child care facilities with the aim of removing them*. Moreover, since young women with children may not be able to accept full-time employment, *the federal government, in association*

with state and local governments, should seek to create part-time public service employment in or near low-income areas so that these young mothers can receive some training and experience in working and earning income, which could be the first step in linking them to the world of work. Many of these young women need information about and access to birth control and family planning services and, in the states where the laws permit, access to facilities for termination of pregnancy. *We recommend that the educational, health, and welfare authorities and other interested public and private organizations cooperate on the design and implementation of effective programs of family planning services and see that they are made available to all young people in the community.*

5. Because there are a large number of dead end jobs in the American economy and because there are barriers that thwart the attempts of workers to move from low-paying to better jobs, we recommend that *all employers—private, nonprofit and government—* on their own, or in association with trade unions and educational and training institutions, *seek to improve the productivity of low-paying jobs through capital investment, jobs redesign, and improved management so that wage rates and earnings can be raised; build career ladders to facilitate the movement of workers from low-paying to better jobs; and provide educational and training opportunities so that poorly paid workers can, by improving their skills, gain access to better jobs in their present or related occupations.*

6. While more and more young blacks are graduating from high school and college, their educational attainments continue to trail those of their white peers. In addition to this competitive disadvantage, many black youths finish high school poorly prepared to enter white-collar employment, particularly jobs that require language and numerical skills. Many words have been written during the past years on where the blame lies. The favorite explanations run the gamut from too little money spent on education through hostile teachers and administrators to lack of parental involvement and support. Putting these explanations to one side, the Task Force underscores its conviction that more effective educational preparation could contribute to easing the employment problems of black youths. To this end we recommend that *more attention be paid to teaching the basic skills of reading and writing in preschool and early school years* through greater parental involvement, more tutoring,

curriculum reform, and other approaches that are found effective. We urge more experimentation with *open schools at junior and senior high school levels so that young people can build on their interests and capacities* rather than follow a rigid curriculum that lacks meaning and relevance for them As in California, *greater use* is indicated of mechanisms whereby *minority youth in college are hired as tutors and counselors to help younger persons* who need assistance in their studies and career planning. *The quality of vocational and technical training* available to high school students and dropouts should be improved through a strengthened system of vocational training, through providing those who are qualified access to selected vocational courses in community colleges and through permitting—indeed encouraging—black youth to enter the more desirable programs.

7. About 40 percent of young people in low-income areas of our cities drop out of junior or senior high school without earning a diploma, and many others obtain a diploma that attests more to their acceptable behavior than to the skill and competence they have acquired. This low ratio of minority youth who graduate with real competence underscores the lack of fit between the educational system and the large numbers of young people it seeks to serve. One important reform would be for employers, labor unions, and the educational authorities to cooperate in bringing about *a substantial expansion of work/study, cooperative, and related programs.* Such programs would take the junior and senior high school student—as well as the junior and senior college student—out of the classroom into the world of work for part of the day, week, month, or term. Although successful cooperative programs require the active participation of employers—and in this connection, government and nonprofit institutions, as well as the private sector, offer potentialities—the major drawback to date has been inadequate funding and poor educational planning and supervision. Cooperative programs will prove beneficial only if they are considered first and foremost as educational programs with work experiences closely related to educational goals and only secondarily as work and income-earning experiences.

8. The states and the federal government passed many statutes in the early 1900's limiting the conditions under which young people and women were permitted to work, the length of the working day

and week, and the equipment they were permitted to handle. With the passage of time, changes in technology, and altered conditions of the workplace, some of this protective legislation has come to impede the employment of young people. We recommend that *the Secretary of Labor initiate a comprehensive review of federal and state legislation and regulations and administrative interpretations of them* as they affect the employment of youth. This review should lead to the provision of revised guidelines for the benefit of legislative and administrative agencies to protect youth from exploitation while broadening their opportunities. Specifically, we recommend that by evaluating the experimental programs currently under way careful consideration be given to lowering the age at which young people are permitted, *as part of an educationally sponsored program, to work at the ages of fourteen or fifteen; to exploring the potentialities of streamlining the issuance of work permits in view of the fact that in 1969 employers used only 42 percent of the 36 million man-hours authorized; and to reassessing whether the broad prohibitions on the use by youth of power machinery is not unnecessarily restrictive under present safety regulations.*

9. Ours may be termed a "credentialed" economy. More and more of the preferred jobs are open only to persons who have acquired the appropriate degree, diploma, certificate, or license. One estimate indicated that in the New York City labor market alone some form of licensing was required for close to a million jobs. Minority youths are kept out of many desirable jobs and career opportunities by educational, certification, and testing requirements that have their roots in discriminatory cultural traditions as well as in employer error or prejudice or professional or trade union efforts to control the labor supply. We recommend that state and local legislative bodies review their licensing structures and procedures *to assure broader representation of public members, including representatives from minority groups; removal of arbitrary obstacles to certification, including high fees for licensing examinations; and restraint in establishing licensing requirements for additional occupations, unless careful study indicates a need.* Further, various leadership groups, such as trade associations, international trade unions, and civil service commissions, *should encourage their constituent organizations to review their formal educational*

requirements for employment with the aim of eliminating requirements that are not work related and that are therefore discriminatory. Finally, employers should give more weight to work experience while credentialing bodies should provide credit for many types of work experience.

10. The manpower training programs financed by the federal government have expanded rapidly since the passage of the Manpower Development and Training Act in 1962. Total federal spending for manpower services approximates $3 billion annually. Of the approximately 1.3 million persons enrolled in these programs in 1970, black youths under twenty-two years of age accounted for about 450,000, or more than 33 percent. We recommend the following changes in manpower programs so that they can contribute more effectively to the employability and career development of black youth. Specifically, *the federal government should link training to a job by providing assurance that a young person who satisfactorily completes a training program and cannot find a position in the private sector because of slack demand will be placed in a public service job where he can add to his skills while earning a wage.* It is destructive to an individual's morale to encourage him to take a training program that does not lead to a job. *The Neighborhood Youth Corps for youth in school should be expanded and planned on a year-round basis as a structured educational-work experience program.* The newly reconstituted Job Corps in urban settings, both residential and nonresidential, *must make special efforts to provide their trainees with useful skills, to place their graduates in jobs, and to follow them up to see whether their costly training is reflected in higher earnings and job advancement.* Because of the high per capita costs in training Job Corps youngsters, it is all the more important to ensure that the training leads to the acquisition of useful skills and employment opportunities.

A hard look at the *Work Incentive Program* is essential. Somewhere from 20 to 25 percent of the mothers receiving some support under the Aid for Families with Dependent Children program are under twenty-four years of age. Moreover, there are many adolescent children in families on welfare. If the Work Incentive Program were to concentrate on improving the employability of these young people, the results might prove more encouraging than the efforts to date.

11. Many young black men and a small number of young black women enlisted during the past two decades in the armed forces to acquire more education and training and to explore whether they might make a career in the military. Since the acceleration of fighting in Vietnam, which coincided with the rise in black consciousness, fewer blacks have looked with favor on the military as an environment in which to seek training or long-term employment. However, under a directive from the Secretary of Defense in 1966, the armed services have drafted or enlisted large numbers of black men who formerly would not have passed military screening requirements. Present military planning contemplates the suspension of the draft by no later than July 1, 1973, and a concurrent substantial reduction in force levels; as a consequence, the armed forces are presently acting to reduce the inflow of low-score men, of whom many are black youth. We recommend that *the armed forces, as the single largest employer in the country, avoid using their prospective personnel stringency as an excuse to reject black youth who, despite low scores, could perform effectively.* We also recommend that when the fighting in Vietnam ceases, *Congress consider a special appropriation to the armed forces for men whom they would not otherwise accept, so that these men can receive training that may be equally beneficial to the reserves and to the civilian economy.* The armed forces have a unique training capability which, in the absence of active fighting, should be used to the maximum.

12. It has long been recognized that poverty and crime are closely linked. The additional tensions under which minorities live, especially in crowded cities, contribute to crimes against persons. When the New York State Advisory Committee to the U.S. Civil Rights Commission held hearings in Harlem a few years ago, the dominant request of local witnesses was for more police protection. The merchants complained bitterly that they had to close their shops before dark because of the danger of burglary. Poor neighborhoods need more and better police protection.

In many low-income areas, young people recognize that the man with money is often involved in illicit or illegal activities—numbers, drugs, prostitution, the resale of stolen goods, racketeering. There is scattered evidence that many young men, probably one to two out of five in urban slum areas, realizing that they have little or no prospect of getting a decent job and earning a decent income, drift into illicit and illegal activities. But those who are apprehended, as well as those who are convicted, need rehabilitation, not punishment. We recommend *more reliance on probation for first offenders with linkage to training and employment programs, such as the Manhattan Court Project in New York City. In addition, appropriate training for those who are sentenced to jail or prison and better placement services after they are released are essential. To this end special efforts must be made not to divulge the sealed proceedings against juveniles and to eliminate questions from employment applications dealing with arrests that did not lead to conviction. Moreover, community leaders should strive to reduce the arbitrary exclusion of former prisoners from many desirable types of employment.* Our present practices with respect to law enforcement are injurious to the community as well as to the delinquent and the criminal.

13. During the 1960's we inaugurated many different experimental and operating programs that impinge on the education, training, and development of young people and seek to broaden their options in the transition from adolescence to adulthood. Many young people, both affluent and poor, have broken out of the institutional confines that have held them prisoner for so long. Street academies, college discovery programs, communes, street people, the Peace Corps, VISTA, and the Teacher Corps suggest the breaking of the mold. But the fact remains that American society lacks the range and variety of developmental opportunities responsive to the unmet needs and changing values of young people during their exploratory years, many of whom remain in school until the age of twenty-four or even later. Young people need a varying diet of education, training, work, income, leisure, and exploration to develop their potential and to help them to find themselves. We have no simple prescription for how these broadened opportunities can be best provided. But we recommend the following lines of action: *easier ways to drop out of school without prejudice and to return to school; more opportunities for young people to enter gainful employment as part of a structured educational and training experience; more governmental and voluntary programs that offer young people opportunities for worthwhile public and community service as part of their educational training and maturational*

development. Young people from affluent homes enjoy many of these broadened options. It is essential that more poor minority youths have similar opportunities. Black youths and other minority youths will face special hardships even if the American people take positive action to turn out urgently needed reforms. They will be frustrated to the point of explosion if the nation fails to fulfill its commitment to them.

BACKGROUND
PAPER

SAR A. LEVITAN is Research Professor of Economics and Director of the Center for Manpower Policy Studies at The George Washington University. He is engaged, under a Ford Foundation grant, in the evaluation of manpower and social welfare programs.

Mr. Levitan has combined academic and government careers. He has taught economics at The State University of New York and The John Hopkins University. As a government economist, he was Research Director of the Senate Special Committee on Unemployment and a consultant to other Congressional committees. Since 1961, he has served as economic consultant to several federal agencies and is presently Vice Chairman of the National Manpower Policy Task Force.

His recent publications include *Antipoverty Work and Training Efforts: Goals and Reality*, 1967; *Federal Training and Work Programs in the Sixties* (coauthor), 1969; *The Great Society's Poor Law: A New Approach to Poverty*, 1969; *Programs in Aid of the Poor for the 1970s*, 1970; *Economic Opportunity in the Ghetto: The Partnership of Government and Business* (coauthor), 1970; *Social Experimentation and Manpower Policy: The Rhetoric and the Reality* (coauthor), 1971; *Blue-Collar Workers* (editor), 1971; and *Big Brother's Indian Programs—With Reservations* (in press), 1971.

He is a graduate of the City College of New York, B.S.S., 1937; and Columbia University, M.A., 1939, Ph.D., 1949.

ROBERT TAGGART III is Executive Director of the National Manpower Policy Task Force.

Mr. Taggart's recent publications include: *Economic Opportunity in the Ghetto: The Partnership of Government and Business* (coauthor), 1970; *Low Income Housing: A Critique of Federal Aid*, 1970; and *Social Experimentation and Manpower Policy: The Rhetoric and the Reality* (coauthor), 1971.

He is a graduate of the College of William and Mary, B.A., 1967, and is completing his doctoral work at The George Washington University.

Most of what we, as outsiders, know about the ghetto has been written by people who are far removed from it in time, distance, income, and culture. Our judgments are usually based on knowledge of other parts of the world. The ghetto's poor are assumed to share the same problems as poor people everywhere; its blacks are assumed to be victimized by the same prejudices as blacks throughout the nation; and its labor markets are assumed to function like those in the mainstream economy. All these assumptions may be wrong to some degree, but no one knows how much. One possible source of error is our tendency to measure the ghetto experience by more familiar standards. Data for the ghetto are collected on the same bases as for the larger community. But their relevance may be questioned; for instance, unemployment and labor force participation rates may have a special meaning where peripheral work patterns are usual and where illicit activities and welfare may be attractive alternatives to work.

Despite the possible weaknesses of such information, there is no substitute for systematic data. Anecdotes and experiences can be found to support almost any argument, but they can hardly be used in creating policy. The only alternative to pure guesswork is to weigh available information, giving due weight to the admitted reservations about its applicability and conditioning the results with insights derived from a wide range of sources and disciplines, in order to create at least a crude picture of ghetto life and its problems.

Moreover, we must attempt to analyze the different aspects of ghetto life over time, finding out how they affect the development of the average individual. This is obviously an elusive ideal. Rigorous data are rarely available; information from diverse sources is usually difficult to integrate; and concentration on a small part of a larger problem can lead to erroneous conclusions.

Recent interest in the ghetto's problems has generated a wealth of information about some aspects of its life. For instance, labor force data collected by the Bureau of Labor Statistics in urban slum areas give a good idea of the comparative success of nonwhites in the world of work, at least to the extent that their activities are comparable to those of youths outside the ghetto. But important gaps remain. Illicit pursuits and the resulting income are generally ignored, though they loom large and threatening in most ghettos. There are almost no reliable data on crime, the income it generates, or its effect on legitimate activities. There is an equal lack of needed data on many other important questions.

Where information is lacking the only recourse is to substitute presumably related data. Though the subject is black youths living in the ghetto, the only available data may deal with nonwhite youths in the city, the Standard Metropolitan Statistical Area (SMSA), or the nation, and in some cases with youths of all races and in all locations. One assumes that the characteristics and behavior of young ghetto blacks are more like those of other young urban blacks than those of blacks in suburban or rural areas; that black ghetto youths are more like nonwhite youths elsewhere than they are like whites; and that they resemble white youths more than they do older people. These assumptions may be misleading, and the use of proxy data may lead to spurious conclusions. But in the absence of specific information, generalized data are the only recourse.

Given all these difficulties and the tentative nature of any assertions about the ghetto, detailed prescriptions for curing the employment problems of young blacks cannot be attained. The complicated picture of reality that emerges from the study reported in the following pages yields no new strategies. Indeed, when the complexities are recognized, many may throw up their hands in despair. Nonetheless, the analysis provides some clues about what should be done. Though reasonable people may differ about the magnitudes of the necessary efforts, the study provides some guidance toward the most promising directions of public policy. Action cannot wait on certainty; if nothing else, the description of the severity of black employment problems should indicate that almost any increased effort is necessary and would be helpful.

This study draws on a number of sources, but perhaps the most important is a longitudinal survey of young whites and nonwhites based on personal interviews. The survey, prepared under a U.S. Department of Labor grant by Dr. Herbert Parnes and his associates of Ohio State University. It contains information not available elsewhere concerning the cumulative aspects of youth problems.

The Current Population Survey employs a stratified sample of households to obtain the monthly employment and unemployment experience of the American population. National data are broken down for all SMSA's with a population of over 250,000. Within these larger SMSA's, further breakdowns are available for poverty neighborhoods, defined as the lowest fifth of census tracts ranked on a scale that considers average income, education, housing, unemployment, and family stability. The Bureau of the Census conducted a more intensive household sampling of six ghetto areas for the Department of Labor in fiscal 1969-70. The Bureau of Labor Statistics designed the study and the Manpower Administration provided the funds. For this "Urban Employment Survey" interviews were conducted with the members (sixteen years of age and over) of 3,600 households in each of six cities—Atlanta, Chicago, Detroit, Houston, Los Angeles, and New York. The sample was selected from neighborhoods singled out for concentrated attention by the U.S. Department of Labor's manpower programs because of their severe poverty and employment problems. The households included in the sample are disadvantaged by almost any measure and are largely nonwhite.

We are indebted to the members of the Twentieth Century Fund Task Force, who supplied careful and critical comments on an earlier draft of this manuscript, and to Drs. Stuart Garfinkle, Bennett Harrison, and Garth L. Mangum. Harvey Hamel of the Bureau of Labor Statistics provided counsel in the use of data and also helped with his comments.

Sar A. Levitan
Robert Taggart III

Memorial Day, 1971

THE
PLIGHT
OF
GHETTO YOUTH

THE RECURRING SYMPTOMS

A decade ago, James B. Conant warned that "the existence in the slums of our large cities of thousands of youths . . . who are both out-of-school and out-of-work is an explosive situation. *It is social dynamite.*"[1] The next eight years witnessed sustained economic growth and rising standards of living accompanied by intensified commitments to improve the quality of education for the poor, to break down the barriers of discrimination and to increase the employability of disadvantaged workers through extensive manpower services. These developments produced real gains, and it seemed for a while that slow but steady progress was being made in attacking the employment problems of ghetto blacks.

Unfortunately the telltale symptoms began to reemerge as economic growth stalled in 1969. By the end of 1970, the serious economic decline had eroded all the ground that had been gained and more. Of 2.4 million nonwhites aged from sixteen to twenty-four in the civilian noninstitutional population in 1960, only 60 percent were looking for or holding jobs, and 18 percent of them were unemployed.[2] In 1970, there were nearly 4 million black youths in the same age bracket, but despite a decline in their labor force participation rate from 61 to 55 percent, their unemployment rate had risen slightly, to 19.4 percent. To make matters worse, the employment status of black youths had deteriorated significantly relative to other groups in the labor force. In 1960, the unemployment rate for nonwhites aged from sixteen to twenty-four was 1.6 times that for all youths; by 1970, it was 1.8 times as high. Over the same period the rate of black youth unemployment increased from 3 to 6 times that for all labor force participants aged twenty-five and over. Teenage blacks also lost ground relative to older blacks, whose employment status improved markedly during the sixties (Chart 1).

The problems of black youths who live in densely populated urban areas are more severe, and their consequences are pervasive. In the hundred largest metropolitan areas there were, in 1970, 1.2 million nonwhite youths aged from sixteen to nineteen and 1.3 million aged from twenty to twenty-four. Among the 40 percent of teenagers in the labor force, 30 percent were unemployed; among the 70 percent of the older youth bracket in the labor force, 13 percent were unemployed. In the poverty areas within these large cities—the areas usually referred to as ghettos, which contain over a million nonwhite youths—conditions are worse still. Although only about 50 percent of all nonwhite youths were in the labor force, some 36 percent of the teenage participants and 15 percent of those aged from twenty to twenty-four were unemployed in 1970.[3] These rates are significantly higher than for white poverty area residents. Young blacks are clearly much worse off than whites or older workers, whether they live in urban areas or the ghettos within these areas (Table 1).

Unemployment is but one of the problems facing black ghetto youths. In almost all dimensions of labor force activity, they are worse off than other youths. Their wages are lower; they work fewer hours; their jobs are less attractive; and their advancement is more limited. Though the statistics that measure these difficulties may not be as accurate for the ghetto as for other areas, they tell a depressing story. And more likely than not, they understate the real problems. Interviewers simply miss many of those who are out of work, and those supported by crime may claim to be working. In either case the number of unemployed would be undercounted. Whatever the inaccuracies of the statistical measures, the differences between the work patterns in the mainstream economy and those of black youth in the ghetto are staggering.

CHART 1.   UNEMPLOYMENT RATIOS, 1948 – 70

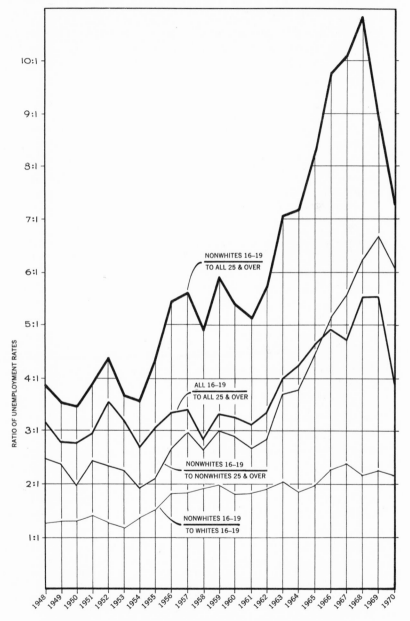

SOURCE: U.S. Department of Labor, Bureau of Labor Statistics.

TABLE 1

**Employment Status of Civilian Noninstitutional Population
by Area, Race, and Age, 1970 Annual Average**

	Civilian Noninstitutional Population	Civilian Labor Force	Labor Force Participation Rate	Unemployment Rate
	(in thousands)		(percent)	
Total U.S.				
Both races				
16 and over	136,995	82,715	60.4	4.9
16-19	14,512	7,246	49.9	15.3
20-24	15,305	10,583	69.1	8.2
Whites				
16 and over	122,112	73,518	60.2	4.5
16-19	12,518	6,439	51.4	13.5
20-24	13,347	9,230	69.2	7.3
Nonwhites				
16 and over	14,883	9,197	61.8	8.2
16-19	1,993	807	40.5	29.1
20-24	1,958	1,354	69.1	13.7
SMSA's over 250,000				
Both races				
16 and over	76,498	46,576	60.9	5.0
16-19	7,805	3,911	50.1	15.8
20-24	8,848	6,182	69.9	8.1
Whites				
16 and over	66,995	40,584	60.6	4.6
16-19	6,616	3,435	51.9	14.0
20-24	7,577	5,302	70.0	7.4
Nonwhites				
16 and over	9,503	5,993	63.1	7.7
16-19	1,190	475	40.0	29.5
20-24	1,271	880	69.2	12.8
Poverty areas in SMSA's Over 250,000				
Both races				
16 and over	10,932	6,202	56.7	7.6
16-19	1,193	541	45.4	24.1
20-24	1,301	876	67.3	11.8
Whites				
16 and over	6,658	3,745	56.2	6.3
16-19	643	326	50.7	16.3
20-24	784	531	67.7	9.4
Nonwhites				
16 and over	4,274	2,457	57.5	9.5
16-19	550	215	39.1	35.8
20-24	517	345	66.7	15.4

Source: U.S. Department of Labor, Bureau of Labor Statistics, Current Population Survey, and Poverty-Non-Poverty Tracts, 1970 (unpublished tabulations).

Though the future of today's youth cannot be predicted with any certainty, it is likely that the employment problems they experience now will have noticeable repercussions tomorrow. Large numbers of ghetto youths are trapped in a secondary labor market where jobs are low-paying and unattractive, advancement opportunities are limited, and training is rarely provided. These jobs are relatively easy to obtain during good times, and they are attractive to youths because of their flexibility. But once a young person accepts these work patterns and adapts his life style to them, he finds it difficult to move into other more demanding areas that might promise a brighter future. While white teenagers also take entry level jobs, they normally have opportunities to move on. Their experience in the secondary labor market is a stepping stone rather than a snare because they are given a chance to develop skills and gain the credentials that provide access to the mainstream economy.

Many black youths nevertheless escape the secondary labor market, only to find that they still must operate on a separate track from whites. Even when they penetrate into more rewarding occupations and industries, they move upward at a slower pace. The problems of these black youths are hidden from view because they take place largely within the employing organization. Blacks and whites of similar education within the same industries and occupations have very different earnings, a fact that points to the existence of separate tracking systems. Because black ghetto youths are caught in secondary labor markets, stranded in entry level jobs far below whites and subject to on-the-job discrimination, the long-term effects on them are conspicuous.

The employment problems of teenagers transcend their unfortunate impact upon the present and future prospects of black youth. The fact that 40 percent of all black teenagers in urban poverty areas are currently unemployed cannot be isolated from such societal ills as rising crime and civil unrest, although the relationships between employment and other social problems cannot be easily established. Careful studies have indicated a significant positive correlation between juvenile delinquency and unemployment.[4] The relationship between illegitimacy and economic opportunity has not been demonstrated, but it is plausible that some women view welfare as the only means to independence when employment opportunities are limited. Finally, there is the fearful possibility that in this time of rising expectations the sudden and drastic increases in ghetto unemployment will lead to another and more severe round of urban riots. Thus the problems of black teenagers are carried over to the rest of the community. The ever-increasing numbers of idle and undirected inner city youths add to the deteriorating quality of urban life.

Although the immediate and long-range implications of youth employment problems are extremely serious, there are positive indices that permit some restrained optimism. For one thing, the demographic outlook is more favorable. The number of young blacks will continue to increase, but the rate of growth will decline. The total number, white and nonwhite, in the fifteen- to twenty-four-year-old age bracket is expected to increase in the 1970's at only half the annual rate of the preceding decade. In the central city these trends will be even more noticeable, reflecting the exodus over the past decade of white families with young children. To the degree that the labor markets have had difficulty absorbing the ever-increasing number of youths and to the extent that blacks have been the most often left out, a slowing rate of expansion may halt the deterioration of conditions.

The social progress achieved on many fronts during the past decade should bear fruit in the years ahead. Whatever the weaknesses of federally funded manpower programs, these efforts concentrate on the needs of black youth, soaking up the unemployed and serving to increase employability for many participants. At the same time, increased income support and improvements in education will heighten the qualifications of blacks entering the labor force. It is also a safe prediction that second and third generation of urban dwellers will be better prepared to meet urban problems than the sons and daughters of rural migrants and consequently more likely to take advantage of available opportunities. Another factor that will have a favorable impact is a decline in birth rates. Contraceptives have reduced unwanted births less among the young than among older women, but their use will become more widespread as youths learn the value of birth control. Finally, advances in reducing discrimination and in providing black adults greater access to the mainstream economy will be self-perpetuating to some degree.

Employers will learn that many of their hiring and promotion practices were ill-conceived and that with modest changes they can tap the reserve of black labor. Blacks who "make it" can help others, at the very least by advising them of available opportunities and providing positive examples. Disappointment over the lack of "instant success" should not be allowed to obscure the very substantial progress that our society has made and the favorable returns that can be expected in the future.[5]

But that is the hopeful future. To date, black youths have benefited little from this progress, and even those gains that they have made have been offset by demographic and economic changes that have made their employment problems more severe. The current economic slump, combined with cutbacks in military enlistments, has accentuated their difficulties in the market place. Only a small minority are able to obtain full-time, relatively stable, and well-paying jobs. As a result, many operate on the periphery of the economy where the boundaries between legitimate and illicit activities are vague. Their negative attitudes and actions are in a large measure the product of their limited opportunities, but they can become self-fulfilling, leading the ghetto youth to ignore the few chances he may have.

For these and many more reasons the employment problems of nonwhite urban youths need to be examined once again to determine their causes, consequences, and cures. Past efforts to solve these problems must be analyzed to determine which were most effective, these must be combined with new strategies, and both must be implemented on a larger scale. For this effort to occur, it must first be recognized that the problems of black ghetto youths are critical. Their deep and pervading causes have not been eliminated and perhaps cannot be for a long time. But the symptoms can be treated to reduce the permanent damage to each wave of black labor force entrants from the ghetto. Those who are ill prepared or who face special obstacles need help so long as the institutions that prepare and utilize their abilities are deficient. Today's nonwhite youths must be given from the outset an equal chance to work and to earn a decent income if the differentials related to the color of one's skin are ever to be ended.

THE SETTING

Economic and Demographic Factors

Though black youths everywhere have severe employment problems, the urban poverty setting intensifies and adds other dimensions to them. Crime, welfare, illegitimacy, overcrowded housing, unstable families, lack of transportation, and population concentration, all a part of central city life, interact to affect employment experiences. Two factors more than any other, however, account for the severity of ghetto economic problems: the rapid growth of black and other minority populations and the movement of industry out of the central city, mainly to the suburbs. The high level of unemployment among all ghetto labor force participants is proof that the supply of workers exceeds, or at least does not match, the demand. The jobs that can be filled by central city residents and are open to them have not increased as rapidly as job seekers. And the major victims of any job deficits are nonwhite urban youths.

The past decades have witnessed a large-scale migration of blacks from rural to urban areas and an equally pronounced emigration of whites from the cities to the suburbs. From 1960 to 1969, the number of central city whites declined by 2.2 million. Over the same period the black population of the central cities increased 3 million; its sixteen- to nineteen-year-old group expanded by 72 percent and the twenty to twenty-four category by 66 percent. As a result, the proportion of nonwhites in the central cities rose from 16 percent to 21 percent over the nine years. In the central cities located in metropolitan areas of more than a million, blacks accounted for an even larger percentage of the population in 1969—30 percent of those aged from sixteen to nineteen, and 24 percent of those from twenty to twenty-four. Altogether there are now an estimated 2 million black youths between the ages of sixteen and twenty-four in our nation's central cities. To complicate matters, the number of white youths has also been growing despite the overall decline in the number of whites. While central city populations rose during the decade by only 1.6 percent (to 58.7 million), the number of all residents between the ages of sixteen to twenty-four increased by more than 25 percent (to 8.8 million).[6]

These trends are likely to continue for some time. Rural migration has not slowed, according to the latest Census figures. The birth rates of nonwhites in central cities are high. The white exodus will probably continue. Consequently it is estimated that nonwhites will increase from 21 to 31 percent of all central city populations between 1969 and 1985. By then, large cities—such as New Orleans, Richmond, Chicago, Philadelphia, St. Louis, Detroit, Cleveland, Baltimore, and Oakland—will join Atlanta, Newark, Gary, and Washington, D.C. as areas whose populations include a majority of blacks.[7] Since the age profile of these black residents is much younger than that of whites, there will be a continuing rapid growth in the black teenage population.

Because of the suburbanization of industry, the expansion in job opportunities for nonwhites has been inadequate to absorb their rapidly increasing numbers. For the past two decades, employment in most large cities has grown at less than the national rate. New and expanding firms have located increasingly in the suburban rings, and many businesses have fled from the problems of the central city. The effects of these changes have been uneven among some industries and occupations so that the employment mix of the central cities has altered.

According to conventional wisdom, the slowed growth in demand for labor and the change in composition have left the central city resident with fewer opportunities for low-skill, entry level work. The real developments, however, are more complex. For instance, a study by Wilfred Lewis revealed that the number of jobs per resident in fifteen large central cities increased between 1959 and 1965.[8] Furthermore, employment in the latter year was more heavily weighted toward low-skill, or at least low-paying, jobs than in the earlier year. Extensions of this analysis to 1968 showed that despite an increasing rate of suburbanization, especially for manufacturing and retail establishments, the number of entry level jobs per central city resident had continued to increase because of the rapid growth in the service and government sectors, which hire many unskilled workers.[9]

The supposition that there has been a net loss of employment opportunities does not explain the high rates of unemployment in the central city. One possibility is that commuters are filling many central city jobs, including some entry level positions. Perhaps more significant, an increased proportion of the resident labor force is competing for the central city's low-skill jobs. As white middle-class families fled to the suburbs and black migrants or those who were poorly educated in urban schools replaced them, the number of competitors for entry level positions increased. Although there has been no absolute loss, the growth in low-skill employment opportunities, limited by suburbanization, has not been enough to match the changes in the composition of the labor force. And since these trends in industrial movement are continuing if not accelerating, central city employment problems will probably intensify. The larger central cities will become predominantly black with heavy concentrations of low-skilled and poorly educated workers. Their jobs will be increasingly in the government and service sectors, but there will not be enough jobs to meet the need.

The Black Youth's Burden

Though urban supply and demand factors strongly affect the employment problems of nonwhite youths, they are not sufficient to explain ghetto employment problems. Young blacks accounted in 1969 for only 5 percent of the total working-age population in all central cities. Since they are an even smaller segment of the labor force, their problems depend not only on aggregate changes in supply and demand but more significantly on how well they compete for available jobs.

All central city residents have problems as a result of suburbanization, but young people, whether white or black, have more difficulties. Because their number has grown rapidly, central city youths have had to compete with older and usually preferred workers for a larger share of the limited number of available jobs. Since black youths are more likely to live in poverty, to occupy substandard housing, to receive a poor education, and to come from a broken home, they are even worse off. All these factors affect their ability to compete with white youths brought up under better circumstances. And whatever their qualifications or abilities, nonwhites have the handicap of their color. Racial discrimination is a pervasive and perverse reality and a major cause of the difficulties of black youths.

It is vital for policy purposes to determine how much each of these factors contributes to the plight of ghetto youths. To the degree that there is a general deficit of jobs in the central city, the only solution to their problems may be to develop urban economies or to stimulate outmigration. To the extent that their difficulties are shared by all who are young, efforts directed to improving the terms and conditions of youth employment could be crucial. If the problems are related to differences in acquired abilities, the preparatory institutions must be improved. And finally, to the degree that nonwhite differentials can only be explained by discrimination in hiring and upgrading, measures must be directed to eliminating these inequities.

One very crude method of estimating the relative importance of these factors is to compare the unemployment rates between the suburbs and the central cities, between younger and older labor force participants within the city, between white and nonwhite youths, and between nonwhites from slum areas and those from more prosperous neighborhoods (Table 2). The largest differential is between the unemployment rate for all central city teenagers and the aggregate rate for the central city; the second largest is between the rate for black and white teenagers. This merely confirms the obvious—that all youths have employment problems and that black youths have the most serious difficulties. The much smaller differentials between slum and nonslum residents, both white and black, suggest that the poverty environment has ill effects but that the color of one's skin alone dramatically affects the chances of employment. If black teenagers were given an equal chance to compete for jobs, especially for those promising stable employment, their unemployment rates would fall substantially.

But this is unlikely to happen unless employment opportunities improve for white as well as black youths. Measures that would increase the openings for young people of all races in the central city would have a major impact on blacks. And these measures, in turn, would probably be ineffective without a healthy central city

TABLE 2

Unemployment Rate Differentials, 1969

	Unemployment Rates
Suburban Rings, 16 and over	3.1
Central City, 16 and over	3.6
Suburban, 16-19	12.1
Central City, 16-19	13.5
Central City White, 16-19	10.6
Central City Black, 16-19	25.1
Slum Area[a] Black, 16-19	27.9
Urban Non-Slum[b] Black, 16-19	22.8
Slum Area[a] White, 16-19	13.8

Ratios

$\dfrac{\text{Central City, All}}{\text{Suburban Ring, All}}$	$\dfrac{3.6}{3.1}$	=	1.16
$\dfrac{\text{Central City, 16-19}}{\text{Suburban Ring, 16-19}}$	$\dfrac{13.5}{12.1}$	=	1.12
$\dfrac{\text{Central City, 16-19}}{\text{Central City, All}}$	$\dfrac{13.5}{3.6}$	=	3.75
$\dfrac{\text{Central City Black, 16-19}}{\text{Central City White, 16-19}}$	$\dfrac{25.1}{10.6}$	=	2.37
$\dfrac{\text{Slum Area Black, 16-19}}{\text{Slum Area White, 16-19}}$	$\dfrac{27.9}{13.8}$	=	2.02
$\dfrac{\text{Slum Area White, 16-19}}{\text{Central City White, 16-19}}$	$\dfrac{13.8}{10.6}$	=	1.30
$\dfrac{\text{Slum Area Black, 16-19}}{\text{Central City Black, 16-19}}$	$\dfrac{27.9}{25.1}$	=	1.11
$\dfrac{\text{Slum Area Black, 16-19}}{\text{Urban Non-Slum Black, 16-19}}$	$\dfrac{27.9}{22.8}$	=	1.22

[a]These data apply to the lowest quartile income tracts in SMSA's with a population of more than 250,000. From Current Population Survey.

[b]These data apply to all areas outside the poverty tracts in SMSA's with a population of more than 250,000. From Current Population Survey.

Source: U.S. Department of Labor, Bureau of Labor Statistics, *Trends in Social and Economic Conditions in Metropolitan and Nonmetropolitan Areas.*

economy. As with most policy matters, the strategies must have as
many facets as the problems. In designing efforts to help black
youths, we must examine the problems they share with all youths to
see what improvements will result if the demand for young workers
can be increased, and we must ascertain the degree of discrimination
and other handicaps that must be removed.

THE EMPLOYMENT PATTERNS

School Attendance and Labor Market Behavior

The basic labor market patterns of black youth are similar to
those of other young people. At age sixteen and seventeen, most are
enrolled in school. Only a minority seeks or holds jobs during the
school year, and its labor force participation is usually confined to
the summer. In the last two teen years about 50 percent are in
school, and only a small proportion of this group works, while the
bulk of out-of-school youths, especially males, are labor force
participants. At age twenty and twenty-one, only 25 percent are
enrolled in school, and more than 45 percent of the remainder are
labor force participants. And by the age of from twenty-two to
twenty-four, more than 66 percent are employed, as almost all males
who are not in school become labor force participants. A larger
percentage of out-of-school females do not seek or hold jobs, largely
because of family responsibilities.

This process of gradual transition between school and work is
illustrated in Chart 2. Nonwhite and white youths go through the
same adjustment process, except that at each juncture the nonwhite
youth is more likely to have graver problems. Whites of all ages have
a higher probability of being in school, and the gap widens as
relatively more pursue higher education. Black male unemployment
rates are higher at all ages, and there is a distinguishable dip in labor
force participation among blacks aged eighteen and nineteen who are
out of school. However, the major interracial differences are in
school attendance patterns. The proportion of nonwhite males in
school is much lower at all ages than that of white youths. The

CHART 2.   EMPLOYMENT AND SCHOOL ENROLLMENT STATUS OF
YOUTHS AGED 16 TO 24, OCTOBER 1969

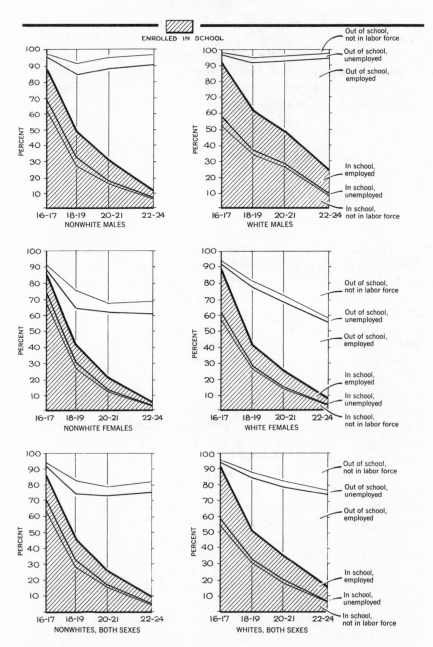

SOURCE: U.S. Department of Labor, Bureau of Labor Statistics.

38

breakdowns by sex reveal several points of interest. Female school enrollment patterns and the work activities of those in school are roughly the same for blacks and whites; but among out-of-school girls, the unemployment rate for blacks is much higher than it is for whites. While labor force participation eventually increases for nonwhite females aged from twenty-two to twenty-four, it declines markedly for whites, suggesting that the former are more likely to work while raising their families.

Because a large proportion of black as well as white youths is enrolled in school, work patterns are highly seasonal. The number of black labor force participants from sixteen to twenty-one years old rose from 1.2 million in February 1970 to 1.7 million in July. This 41 percent increase in the number seeking jobs was not absorbed, and the number of unemployed rose from 255,000 to 449,000, an increase of more than 75 percent. Similar seasonal patterns occur for white youths, but they are much less pronounced. Between February and July 1970, the number of white labor force participants in the same age bracket rose by 33 percent, while the number of unemployed increased by only 40 percent.[10] Thus a smaller proportion of white youths seeks summer employment, and a far larger percentage of these finds jobs.

The same seasonal pattern occurs in the ghetto. During the summer months, the proportion of labor force participants increases dramatically (Chart 3). Since jobs are not available to absorb all these would-be workers, unemployment rates, especially for girls, rise. These seasonal fluctuations, however, are not as marked for nonwhites in slum areas as they are for nonwhites elsewhere.

The seasonal labor force pattern partly accounts for the high rates of youth unemployment. There is often an unavoidable period of unemployment associated with job search during entry or reentry into the work force. The duration of idleness depends on the availability of jobs, the adequacy of the search, and the effectiveness of institutional arrangements made to match job seekers and job openings. The longer it takes each entrant to find work, the higher the average unemployment rate. No matter what the cause of unemployment, the slum youth is likely to be unemployed longer, with 44 percent out of work for five or more weeks compared with 37 percent of all youths (Table 3).

CHART 3.   MONTHLY EMPLOYMENT STATUS, 1970,
          OF 16–21-YEAR-OLD NONWHITE MALES AND FEMALES
          IN POVERTY AREAS WITHIN SMSA'S OVER 250,000

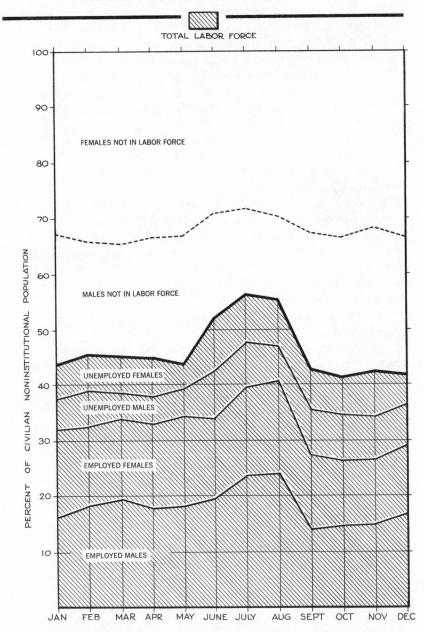

SOURCE: U.S. Department of Labor, Bureau of Labor Statistics,
        Current Population Survey, "Poverty–Non-poverty Tracts" (unpublished tabulations, 1970).

TABLE 3

**Unemployment by Duration and Cause for
16-19-Year-Old Youths, July 1968-June 1969**

	Less Than 5 Weeks	5-14 Weeks	15 and Over	Percent of Teenage Labor Force	Percent of Teenage Unemployment
Total					
All youths	63.2	29.0	7.8	12.2	100.0
Six city slums	56.1	31.1	12.8	29.6	100.0
Lost job					
All youths	66.1	24.4	9.5	1.8	14.8
Six city slums	60.0	25.7	14.2	3.7	12.5
Left job					
All youths	73.0	22.0	5.0	1.4	11.7
Six city slums	63.1	22.7	14.1	3.6	12.2
New entrants					
All youths	59.9	32.2	7.8	4.8	38.9
Six city slums	57.5	31.8	10.7	9.9	33.4
Reentrants					
All youths	61.8	29.7	8.4	4.2	34.7
Six city slums	51.7	34.7	13.6	12.4	41.9

Source: U.S. Department of Labor, Bureau of Labor Statistics.

Peripheral Workers

Both white and nonwhite youths are "peripheral" workers—characterized by intermittent or part-time, low-income employment, concentrated in the low-status industries and occupations. Only 13.1 percent of employed nonwhite teenagers in the six urban slums in fiscal 1969 and 8.7 percent of white teenagers nationally in 1968 worked on a full-time, full-year basis (Table 4). More than 50 percent of the white teenagers and 33 percent of the blacks worked part time. The differences result from the higher percentage of blacks out of school and the greater likelihood that those in school will seek full-time summer employment.

Because of their seasonal, part-time and intermittent work patterns as well as their lack of skills and experience, and because

TABLE 4

Work Experience of 16-19-Year-Olds and Total Labor Force

	Nonwhites 16-19 in Six-City Slum Area Sample, 1969	Total 16-19 1968	Total Labor Force 1968
Work experience	37.6	33.2	32.4
Worked			
Primarily full-time			
(more than 35 hours)	64.6	44.2	81.2
50-52 weeks	13.1	8.7	57.9
40-49	5.8	2.7	7.3
27-39	7.7	3.9	5.1
14-26	13.0	9.4	5.2
1-13	25.0	19.6	5.8
Primarily part-time			
(less than 35 hours)	35.4	55.8	18.8
50-52 weeks	5.9	14.5	6.4
40-49	3.4	3.9	2.0
27-39	3.5	6.3	2.2
14-26	6.9	11.4	3.3
1-13	15.5	19.5	5.0

Source: U.S. Department of Labor, Bureau of Labor Statistics.

they are often left no other choice, teenagers are concentrated in different industries and occupations from older workers. Until they reach their twenties, only a small proportion develop "stable" work patterns or are willing to make the commitments needed to rise above their entry level positions. At the same time, many employers who have never hired young people are reluctant to do so because they believe them to be undependable; this excludes young workers who might prove to be productive and stable. There is thus both a pull and a push toward employment in what has been labeled a secondary labor market where jobs are low-paying, turnover rates are high, training is meager, and opportunities for advancement are limited. White and nonwhite teenagers are more likely than older workers to be employed in the service and retail sectors. Black youths are more likely than their white counterparts to be employed in the public sector or in manufacturing and are less likely to work in the retail sector. Occupationally, nearly 90 percent of nonwhite youths in the large SMSA poverty neighborhoods are clerical workers, operatives, or service workers, as are 80 percent of white teenagers throughout the SMSA; by comparison, a little more than 50 percent of all the nation's workers fall in similar occupational categories.

Because they are entry level workers concentrated in the lower-paying industries, the average wage of both black and white youths is low, and nonwhite youths receive less for their labors than whites. This is demonstrated in a comparison of 1967 hourly earnings for males in urban poverty areas:[11]

Age	White	Nonwhite
15-17	$1.59	$1.53
18-19	1.93	1.75
20-25	2.78	2.14

According to another survey, 28 percent of black but only 18 percent of white out-of-school females between the ages of 18 and 24 earned less than $1.50 per hour in 1968.[12]

Intermittent work patterns further depress weekly and yearly earnings. In the six large city slums, where only 13 percent of nonwhite teenagers work full-year full-time, the fiscal 1969 median income of this minority was only $3,677 for males and $3,339 for females. In the average week, nearly 33 percent of those teenage slum residents who were working reported earnings of less than $50 and an additional 40 percent earned between $50 and $75.[13] Obviously, few of these youths are earning enough to support a family or even to support themselves adequately.

Dropouts and Discouraged Workers

Youths who are neither employed nor looking for work are an object of special concern. It is widely asserted that more and more young people, especially in the ghettos, are becoming alienated from the work system and spurn employment at any reasonable wage. It is important to get some perspective on this alleged phenomenon. According to the six-city slum survey, 36 percent of all sixteen- to twenty-one-year-old nonwhite males and 50 percent of the females were not in the labor force in fiscal 1969. Of these males, 70 percent, and of these females, nearly 50 percent did not seek work because they were in school. An additional 40 percent of the females stayed out of the labor force because they were keeping house. While there is no doubt that many outside the labor force could obtain and might want gainful employment, they are mostly occupied in useful pursuits. Whatever the exact number of economic dropouts and street corner hustlers, they seem to be equally distributed among black and white youths. In 1969, 14 percent urban white and poverty area nonwhite teenagers were outside the labor force for reasons other than school attendance, housekeeping, and physical disability. These statistics undoubtedly understate the problem, since many youths who are out in the street may not be counted and many who are nominally in school are on the street. It is clear, however, that a vast majority of young blacks, even in the worst ghettos, are trying to make a successful adjustment to the world of work, as are white youths.

The visibility of street corner hustlers and concern with their activities should not obscure the employment problems of the much larger number who want jobs and earnings. While there may be many who drop out of the labor force to pursue less "respectable" activities, there are also many who drop out because they are discouraged. These youths would take jobs if they were offered, but they are not looking because they have little hope of finding them or have some other temporary difficulty. Nearly 50 percent of all nonwhites aged from sixteen to twenty-four in the six-city survey who were not in the labor force in fiscal 1969 said they wanted a job. It is obvious that a large proportion who are not looking for jobs might be coaxed into the labor market if opportunities were more plentiful.

The fact that nonwhite youths have more severe problems than whites at each step of their adjustment to the world of work suggests that the causes lie all along the transition process. There is no single point in time, no single dimension of their difficulties that is responsible. Instead, there are inadequacies in almost all the formal and informal mechanisms of adjustment, and these interact cumulatively. The frequently cited liturgy of woes is as familiar as it is depressing: many nonwhite families lack the resources to provide motivation or preparation for employment; central city schools are typically inferior and do little to develop the abilities of black students; dropout rates are high as youths become discouraged with their education or desperately need job income; the ghetto labor market mechanisms are ineffective in many ways, denying nonwhite youth information about attractive opportunities; the mobility of ghetto youth is limited by the lack of personal and public transportation and by housing discrimination; a substantial minority of black girls have children at an early age, finding welfare the only recourse; black males, if drafted into military service, receive little valuable training they can use upon discharge; and finally, discrimination limits employment and advancement opportunities at all stages.

Each of these factors must be examined for validity, cause, and possible cure of the problems it creates, since each contributes to the disabling work experiences of black ghetto youths. However, the separate factors are largely inseparable. Occupational distribution affects unemployment rates, income, mobility, advancement opportunities, and much more, and this distribution is the result of discrimination, deficient labor market information, inadequate training opportunities, and many other factors. These variables are related over time, with cumulative effects. The classic example is the argument used by employers to rationalize their discrimination practices: the nonwhite youth is undependable, poorly educated, unmotivated or unskilled. The employer may have many legitimate reasons for turning down the nonwhite applicant; his own discrimination may be only marginal, making but a small contribution to the applicant's disadvantages. Nonetheless the incidence of employment discrimination together with the numerous inadequacies on other fronts become major handicaps.

It should thus be clear that these causes and the problems they create must be analyzed from a longitudinal perspective. Their interrelationships and the cumulative nature of their impacts must be understood to gain insights into the difficulties of black youths and the probable effectiveness of alternative strategies for their elimination.

NOTES

1. National Committee for Children and Youth, *Social Dynamite* (Washington, D.C.: the Committee, 1961), p. 26. Emphasis supplied.

2. U.S. Department of Labor, *Manpower Report of the President, 1970* (Washington, D.C.: Government Printing Office, March 1970), pp. 217-32.

3. U.S. Department of Labor, Bureau of Labor Statistics, Current Population Survey, "Poverty-Non-Poverty Tracts" (unpublished tabulations, 1970).

4. The President's Commission on Law Enforcement and Administration of Justice, *Juvenile Delinquency and Youth Crime* (Washington, D.C.: Government Printing Office, 1970), pp. 308-9.

5. Eli Ginzberg and Dale L. Hiestand, *Mobility in the Negro Community* (Washington, D.C.: Government Printing Office, June 1968).

6. U.S. Department of Commerce, Bureau of the Census, *Trends in Social and Economic Conditions in Metropolitan and Nonmetropolitan Areas,* Current Population Reports, series P-23, no. 33 (Washington, D.C.: Government Printing Office, September 1970), pp. 11-12.

7. National Commission on Urban Problems, *Building the American City* (Washington, D.C.: Government Printing Office, 1968), p. 43.

8. Wilfred Lewis, Jr., "Urban Growth and Suburbanization of Employment—Some New Data" (Washington, D.C.: The Brookings Institution, 1969; mimeographed), p. 17.

9. Robert Taggart III, "The Suburbanization of Employment" (Washington, D.C.: Center for Manpower Policy Studies, The George Washington University, 1970; mimeographed).

10. *Employment and Earnings,* March and August 1970, table A-5.

11. U.S. Department of Labor, *Youth Unemployment and Minimum Wages,* Bulletin 1657 (Washington, D.C.: Government Printing Office, 1970), p. 102.

12. John Shea *et al., Years for Decision,* vol. 1 (Columbus, Ohio: Center for Human Resource Research, The Ohio State University, 1971), table 5.10.

13. U.S. Department of Labor, Bureau of Labor Statistics, "Urban Employment Survey" (unpublished tabulations).

THE FORMATIVE YEARS

From the day he is born, the black male in the ghetto is exposed to familial, institutional, and economic influences that tend to limit his ability to compete in the world of work with others from more affluent and stable circumstances. Before he reaches his teens, when work experience usually begins, the black manchild is already disadvantaged in many respects.

Broken Homes and Poverty

One of the many factors that impede his development is the substantial possibility of coming from a broken home. In the central cities, 30 percent of all nonwhite families had a female head in 1969, compared with only 12 percent of white families. More than 75 percent of the families headed by a black female had children, and 54 percent had two or more. In comparison, less than 50 percent of the white families headed by a female had children, and only 27 percent had two or more.

These children from broken homes face special obstacles, though many are able to overcome them with little apparent difficulty. The most obvious obstacle is poverty. More than 50 percent of all nonwhite families headed by females in metropolitan areas have an income below the government's poverty standards.[1]

Central city youths who grow up in stable homes still must face many difficulties. Low income, typical even in families in which the husband and wife are present, limits opportunities. For instance, both parents may have to work, though parental attention is needed at home unless outside child care is available. In the central cities, 3.2 million of the 12.5 million blacks were poor in 1968, and 33 percent of all youths under eighteen years of age lived in poverty. The median income for all nonwhite families, which averaged 4.1 members, was only $6,139, providing a minimal life style in most urban areas.[2]

A large proportion of nonwhite families is also on welfare, and many youths have no successful work example in the home. It is estimated that more than 20 percent of all families in the six large city slums surveyed by the Department of Labor were public assistance recipients in fiscal 1969, and the proportion is rising. Most of these families are headed by females and rely on AFDC, adding the negative effect of dependency to the lack of a paternal influence. Though statistical proof is lacking, it is a safe assumption that to some degree welfare begets welfare by engendering attitudes of dependency in the children who grow up on the public dole.

Even in families with a working head the example set may not be one to warrant emulation. Many family heads work in dead end, low-paying jobs, with frequent intervals of unemployment and little commitment to employment. Their disappointments are bound to be communicated to their children, who in turn may reject not only work but also the parents they see as failures. With this example a black youth is far less likely to depend on his parents for occupational advice than is a white youth.[3]

Peer Group Influences

The negative influences in the home are often compounded by equally negative peer group contacts. Acclimated to life on the street at an early age, the black boy may view as heroes those who "make it" through illegitimate activities. These examples often lead in adolescence to experiments with such offenses as skipping school, which may escalate to minor crime and violence.

The frequency of crime is alarmingly high for all age groups in the ghetto. Young children are bound to have fairly close contact with someone who has been arrested, since it is estimated that between 50 and 90 percent of all males have serious encounters with the police by the time they reach the age of twenty-five.[4] This kind of experience rubs off, setting the style for youngsters, of whom a large number commit crimes even before they work. Between 25 and 50 percent of the 506,000 youths arrested during 1969 in urban areas were black, and probably 90 percent were males.[5] The arrest rate for robbery in 1967 was 27 per 100,000 for white youths aged from ten to seventeen, while for young blacks, the rate was 549.7 per 100,000.[6] Granted that black youths may be much more likely to be arrested for crimes than whites, the massive differences are not explained by the many uncertainties underlying the gathering and use of arrest statistics. Since arrests account for less than 20 percent of the crimes that youths are likely to commit, and since many illicit acts are not even reported, the incidence of adolescent crime in the ghetto is undeniably high.

Even if he does not participate in criminal acts, the young black male is influenced by the life around him. Before he reaches working age, he will realize that there are alternatives to hard and unrewarding work in school or on the job. To some degree, early transgressions and the asocial behavior expressed in vandalism and disruptive conduct are harmless—boys will be boys. But too often, observation of adolescent crime or participation in it may influence the motivation and shape the outlook of the ghetto youth, affecting his future choices between school and work and illicit activities.

Poor Schools

Adding to the negative influence at home and in the streets, the schools attended by the black male are generally inferior or are at least unable to make up for his other problems. By the time he reaches the ninth grade he is appreciably behind whites of the same age. Achievement tests are unquestionably biased against those who grow up in the ghetto, but they cannot be totally disregarded. The tests show that nonwhite ninth graders in northeastern metropolitan areas are 2.4 grades behind white youths in verbal achievement and 2.8 years behind in math; in other geographical areas, the differentials are even greater.[7]

There are many reasons for this low achievement. As experience with the Head Start program has shown, children from poor families with uneducated parents are far behind their more fortunate peers by the time they enter school, especially in verbal and communicative skills. The schools they attend are often run-down, with ancient equipment and outdated texts. Their teachers are often less experienced and less qualified, since many central cities have few options in selecting teachers to fill their staffs. Most of all, the peer group influence in school can be negative when deprived children come in contact only with other deprived children.

Crime and absenteeism are problems even in ghetto grammar schools, and a minority of disruptive students can create an atmosphere in which teaching and learning become extremely difficult. Slow learners are usually passed from grade to grade despite their lack of achievement because resources to provide individual attention are lacking. By the time such youths are "promoted" to high school, much of what is taught is over their heads. The better students find classwork boringly easy, and academic potential is often ignored by peers and teachers. Thus both the slow and fast learners are likely to be dissatisfied and ready to drop out of school at the earliest possible date, especially if they feel that additional education will have little influence on their future work.

By the time the nonwhite ghetto youth reaches working age, he has several handicaps hindering his adjustment to the world of work. Negative family, peer group, and institutional influences will have to be corrected if ghetto youths are to start their work careers with a chance equal to that of whites. Admittedly, it will take a long time to correct these deficiencies. Until they can be corrected, efforts must be directed toward helping youths who have grown up in broken homes, who have experimented with crime, who have developed asocial tendencies, and who are poorly educated. Experience has shown that improvements are possible despite those handicaps, and that white-nonwhite employment differentials can be reduced significantly even for those who have grown up with the disadvantages of ghetto life.

THE YEARS OF TRANSITION BETWEEN
SCHOOL AND WORK

Experimentation in the Early Teens

The earliest employment experiences usually begin at the ages of fourteen and fifteen, though some youths may begin working sooner. About 10 percent of nonwhites of these ages are in the labor force in September; 30 percent at the seasonal peak in July. Compulsory school attendance keeps all but 5 percent of this age group in school, and child labor laws confine those in the labor force to very marginal jobs even if better opportunities are available.

Ghetto males from fourteen to fifteen years of age may also begin to pursue illicit activities for profit as street life takes on economic significance. From thirteen to fifteen, arrests are high for property crimes as well as for youthful offenses, such as disorderly conduct, vandalism and running away from home. White and nonwhite youths of this age group accounted for 11.2 percent of all arrests in 1969, but 26.8 percent of those for burglary, larceny, and auto theft. Since 40 percent of blacks under eighteen who are arrested are charged with property crimes, compared with 30 percent of young white offenders, it is obvious that many youths are supplementing their incomes, or at least meeting some of their consumer desires, through petty crime.[8] A large percentage of these offenders are probably apprehended because of their lack of skill in the "art" of crime.

But the primary activity of black youths in their early teens is school, and work or crime are usually only part-time and peripheral economic activities pursued by a minority. In school, important decisions are being made about educational and occupational goals as inflated childhood expectations are adjusted to realistic possibilities. According to one study, 45 percent of fourteen- and fifteen-year-old black students revised their educational aspirations downward, compared with only 25 percent of those aged sixteen and seventeen.[9] It is thus at fourteen or fifteen that most nonwhite males decide whether to commit themselves to continuing their education.

If they make a positive decision, they tend to cling tenaciously to their high expectations; if they decide that school is not for them, the period until they can legally drop out is characterized by high rates of absenteeism and little educational progress. This tendency explains why in central city schools, such as those in Washington, D.C., more than 20 percent of the high school students are absent every day.

The change in educational expectations is reflected in the choice of high school curriculum. Blacks are more likely than whites to choose—or to have chosen for them—vocational, commercial, or general programs of study. Less than 25 percent of all black youths are in college preparatory courses, compared with almost 50 percent of the whites. Nevertheless, 50 percent of the fourteen- and fifteen-year-old nonwhite youths in school say they expect to go to college. This is unrealistic in light of the fact that less than 40 percent of those who graduate from high school enroll in college.[10]

School or Work?

The sixteenth year is crucial, since this is usually the age at which school attendance is no longer required and many of the work restrictions under child labor laws end. The option thus expands to drop out of school to work full time. The proportion of blacks who are out of school increases from 5 percent for fourteen- and fifteen-year-olds to 25 percent among sixteen- and seventeen-year-olds.[11] The dropouts are usually far behind standard in their academic achievement; they are from lower-income homes in which they have little exposure to reading materials or learning experiences; and their parents are likely to be unemployed or working in low-status occupations.[12] Some analysts assert that they can calculate from these factors alone a fifth grader's chances of dropping out without graduating from high school.

Some youths, however, take account of their chances of immediate employment and earnings in making their decision about dropping out of school. One cross-sectional analysis showed a correlation between the level of unemployment in cities and school retention: for each percentage point that unemployment rates exceeded the national average, enrollment rates of males aged sixteen and seventeen were one percentage point higher.[13] In other words, the more jobs there are for teenage males, the more likely they are to leave school.

Nearly 80 percent of all nonwhite sixteen- and seventeen-year-old males who were out of school in October 1969 sought or held jobs.[14] Among all these dropouts, but especially among 20 percent who were not participating in the labor force, crime rates were high. At ages sixteen and seventeen, burglary, larceny, and auto theft arrests tend to decrease but arrests for narcotics violations, disorderly conduct, and violent crime increase. These facts apparently reflect increased alienation and rebellion rather than the pursuit of crime for income. It is doubtful that many youths in this age group can make more money in crime than they can by work; so the vast majority hold jobs with only intermittent illicit activities to supplement income.

At the Crossroads

At the age of eighteen or nineteen, most black males leave school, either graduating or dropping out, swelling the number of those who are out of school and competing for jobs. More than 50 percent of the nonwhite males in this age bracket were not enrolled in school in October 1969, and the proportion increases to 70 percent for those aged twenty and twenty-one.[15]

Many dropouts give up in their last years of school. A survey of black slum residents in Roxbury, Central Harlem, Bedford-Stuyvesant, North Philadelphia, East St. Louis, and Mission Philmore, San Francisco, showed that the proportion of twenty-year-olds who had completed high school ranged between 30 and 52 percent. For those aged from twenty to twenty-four, the rates rose to between 53 and 72 percent, as many apparently earned diplomas in the military or in adult education courses.[16]

Those who remain in school until their late teens are typically far behind whites in attainment and achievement. One sample showed that among twelfth graders, 87 percent of whites are younger than eighteen, compared with only 79 percent of blacks.[17] The differences in achievement are even more striking. By the twelfth grade, the nonwhite in the northeast is 3.3 grades behind the white student in verbal ability and 2.9 grades in reading; in mathematics he is operating at the level of the seventh grade white student.[18] Data from other tests, such as armed forces qualification exams, corroborate these substantial differences. While a certain bias in achievement tests leads to these lower scores, most of the difference is real; for instance, it is unlikely that there is much cultural bias in arithmetic achievement tests.

For those who graduate from high school, one of the most vital questions is whether or not to go to college. The majority, including a large proportion who had expected to attend college even in their senior year, find the obstacles insurmountable. Only 38 percent of blacks who were seniors in 1966 were still in school in 1967 as compared with 64 percent of whites.[19] This differential is highly significant, since college is the prime vehicle for upward mobility. The reasons that fewer blacks attend college are complex. Low income is only one reason, albeit a highly significant one. Environmental factors also reduce the nonwhite's drive toward higher education. His lack of exposure to reading materials and the low educational attainment of his parents may provide little stimulus, adding to a growing built-in sense of failure. The fact that college may offer fewer benefits for him than it does for the white youth is another factor. If his decisions are based on economic factors, he may decide that the lower return will not justify the investment of time and money.

THE UNCERTAIN YEARS—TAKING THE TURN

Military Service

For eighteen- and nineteen-year-olds who are not deferred for higher education, the draft becomes a significant factor. Some youths see the military as a chance for self-improvement when they leave school and enlist voluntarily, but most wait to be drafted. The widespread belief that black youths are more likely than whites to enter the service is untrue, and only in the past few years have the black youth's chances of military service been as high as the white's. Although blacks accounted for 12.1 percent of the male population in the prime draft years between eighteen and twenty-five, black men comprised only 8.7 percent of the armed forces at the end of 1969. This overstates the relative proportion of youths who serve, since the average nonwhite serviceman is more likely to reenlist than the white and a larger proportion of those in service have served more than a single tour.[20]

Nonwhites are less likely to volunteer or to pass the selective service examination if they are called. In 1968, the ratio of enlistees to draftees was 56 to 44 for nonwhites, compared with 65 to 35 for whites. Among youths given a preinduction examination in 1969, only 44 percent of the blacks were found acceptable, compared with 57 percent of the whites. About 33 percent of the nonwhites who were disqualified had medical disabilities, 53 percent failed the mental test, and 11 percent failed both. At the induction examination, more nonwhites were disqualified—18.1 percent compared with 15.1 percent for whites. However, since whites are more likely to enlist and since quotas are set by area without taking into account the proportion of rejectees, blacks are overrepresented among those who are drafted. In 1968, the 42,000 blacks drafted accounted for 14.3 percent of those of all draftees; only 55,000 blacks enlisted, or 10.6 percent of the total of all enlistees. Overall, 11.9 percent of those going into the service were nonwhites, a higher proportion than in previous years.[21]

These data suggest that a relatively large proportion of nonwhites do not meet even the minimal requirements of military service and that those who are qualified are not able to exploit the loopholes in the induction procedures used by whites from more affluent families, such as deferral for college education. Investigations of preinduction physical examinations show that rejectees are likely to come from poor nonwhite families, to have been unemployed before examination, to have dropped out of school, and to have had encounters with the law.[22] Since all these characteristics are shared by a sizable portion of the black youth population, disqualification rates are probably high in the ghettos. On the other hand, few of those who qualify are able to avoid service through deferment. The armed forces skim the cream of the ghetto population, leaving behind those who are unacceptable by even the low military standards. These rejects are the least likely to have favorable employment experiences.

The armed forces have long maintained that the skills acquired in military service enhance the employability of veterans. Regrettably, there is little evidence to support this claim. During 1969, 19 percent of the nonwhite males aged from twenty to twenty-four in the civilian noninstitutional population were veterans (compared with 25 percent of the whites of this age). The unemployment rate for nonwhite veterans was 10.0 percent, compared with 8.1 percent among nonveterans of the same age and race; for white veterans the rate was 5.1 percent compared with 4.5 percent for nonveterans.[23] That is, the ratio of veteran to nonveteran unemployment rates was 1 to 2 for blacks and 1 to 1 for whites.

A more specific study of veterans living in low-income neighborhoods—more than 80 percent of whom were between the ages of twenty and twenty-five—indicated that black youths benefit less from military service than whites, even when both are from disadvantaged backgrounds.[24] The employment experience of blacks was noticeably inferior to that of whites; 9.9 percent were unemployed, 4.6 percent were not in the labor force, and the employment status of 3.5 percent was not ascertained. Among whites, only 2.6 percent were unemployed and 3.6 percent were not in the labor force, while the employment status was not ascertainable for only 1.2 percent. The mean weekly earnings of blacks was $122.53 compared with $134.18 for whites. While 56 percent of the whites felt their chances of promotion in their jobs were good, only 47 percent of the blacks expected promotion. At the other end of the attitude spectrum 29 percent of the whites were pessimistic about job advancement, compared with 40 percent of the blacks. Fewer blacks than whites, about one in four, had participated in military education programs. Only 11 percent of blacks with jobs were using any of their military skills or training in their work, and only 8 percent of the blacks were currently enrolled in formal education or training, compared with more than 20 percent of the whites. The study raises doubts about the frequently asserted salutary effects military service is presumed to exercise for the ghetto blacks who actually get into the armed services.

However, if military service is of little advantage to veterans, it undoubtedly helps those who remain at home. The stepped-up military demands between 1965 and 1969, combined with an increased effort to draft the disadvantaged, removed many youths from the ghetto labor force, reducing job competition for those who did not serve. At the beginning of the Vietnam escalation in 1965, there were 2.7 million persons in the armed forces; by late 1968, there were 3.6 million, an increase of about 900,000 men, most of them eighteen to twenty-four years old. This rise in the armed forces strength is estimated to have accounted for more than 25 percent of the reduction in aggregate unemployment rates between 1964 and 1969, on the assumption that there would have been about 500,000 more persons in the civilian labor force in 1969 without the Vietnam buildup.[25]

Unfortunately the sword cuts both ways. Present and planned reductions in military manpower levels have dire implications for black youth. At the end of 1970 there were 3 million persons in the armed services, a decline of 600,000 from the late 1968 peak. The number is expected to continue to decline to around 2.5 million by the end of 1971. The result will be to reverse the employment gains of the Vietnam buildup. If the siphoning off of labor force participants caused a substantial decline in unemployment among black eighteen- to twenty-four-year-olds, an equal increase in the civilian labor force should, all else remaining the same, result in more than a substantial increase in their unemployment. This was indeed the case in 1969 and 1970.

Looking and Loafing

Black youths who have left school and are not inducted into the armed forces have a choice of working or taking to the streets, many combining the two. High school graduates seeking work want more rewarding employment than they found on a part-time or intermittent basis during school. Dropouts who may have more work experience are also looking for better-paying and stable jobs. For most male youths, the late teens are a period of active search, with experimentation in different jobs interspersed with stretches of watching and waiting without employment.

Black youths use the same methods of job hunting as whites. They are slightly more likely to use public employment agencies, but those who do account for only a small minority of placements. Most positions are found through direct contact with an employer or referral by a friend or relative; in the six slum areas in fiscal 1969, 60 percent of the working teenagers used one of these two methods to find their current job. However, direct contact and personal referral are less effective for blacks than for whites. Since a smaller proportion of black applicants is accepted for most jobs, according to employer surveys, this avenue of search is often unrewarding.[26] Direct contacts are usually limited to the area of residence; so ghetto youths have little likelihood of finding the better jobs available in the cities and the suburbs. Since the black youth's friends or relatives probably work in unattractive and low-paying jobs, he is likely to be channeled into similarly unrewarding work. On the other hand, these methods of search would probably work if there were no inequities in the job market or in the preparatory institutions. Improving labor market mechanisms through the introduction of more efficient placement services can make only a marginal contribution so long as these other problems exist. Black as well as white youths would be better off if they had the information and counseling to make more rational occupational choices. But the exploratory period is part of growing up; though it can be shortened somewhat, it cannot be eliminated. The difference is that whites can move upward while blacks are more frequently blocked by lack of opportunities. If these were more readily available, it is likely that black youths would adjust the scope of their search.

For white as well as black youths in this period of testing and search or waiting around for the draft, economic necessity is not a prime motivation. The large majority of nonwhite eighteen- and nineteen-year-old males live at home; in 1966, only 12 percent were married and supporting families.[27] At the same time, life on the street is attractive because of freedom, adventure, and, occasionally, high rewards. It is not surprising that at this age there is a marked increase in the number of youths who are not in school and not in the labor force. In poverty areas of SMSA's with populations over 250,000, more than 25 percent of all nonwhite males from eighteen to nineteen years of age were not in the labor force for some reason other than health, housekeeping responsibilities, or school attendance. And though more than 60 percent of ghetto males of this age group are labor force participants, there is probably a high rate of exit and reentry, with a large majority of youths experiencing life on the street at one time or another.

Because illicit activities can be an attractive alternative to work and because few youths have family responsibilities, many are not interested in taking jobs that pay low wages and have little status. When unemployment rates were at a low in 1969 and jobs were relatively plentiful, it proved to be difficult in many cities to recruit eighteen- and nineteen-year-old youths for public employment programs at minimum wage rates, even though unemployment for males of this age continued to be high.[28] Yet the belief that a large proportion of out-of-school youths of this age have "unreasonable" employment expectations is not supported by available evidence. According to the study of poverty neighborhoods of six major cities, the mean required wage for unemployed youth was lower than what was being earned by those who were employed. The only significant example of inflated wage expectations was among nonwhites eighteen- and nineteen-years old. While nearly 38 percent of those who worked earned less than $1.40 per hour in 1967, only 29 percent of the unemployed were willing to take a job at this wage. Still, the mean required wage for this group was lower than the mean received by those who worked.[29]

This limited evidence does not disprove the notion held by many employers that youths are reluctant to work at the going wage. For one thing, there may be many low-wage jobs that are acceptable and others that are not. A teenager may be willing to work at less than the minimum wage in an office but not as an orderly. Similarly, because those who are unemployed and out of the labor force may be less qualified, the going wage for their services may be lower than that of the employed.

Nevertheless, the evidence suggests that the majority of teenage males have realistic wage expectations. Claims to the contrary are often based on misconceptions. A large number of young males move in and out of work both voluntarily and involuntarily; when they are out of money, when hustling is not productive, or when the "heat" is on, they may be willing to take a low-wage job they would spurn the Monday after payday. With money in their pockets, they can afford leisure and can wait around for the occasional opportunities to earn good money for a short time, either through work or illicit activities. Their attitudes toward work, labor force participation, and street corner activities depend largely on their financial state.[30] But their attitudes also depend on the availability and attractiveness of employment opportunities. The sharp increase in nonwhite youth employment that occurred during the tight labor markets of 1967-69 should dispel the fears of a "backward bending" labor supply curve—one where increased wages lead to less work. The choice between leisure, crime, and work is rational in the sense that increasing wages and employment opportunities will lure teenagers off the street and out of trouble. Many will continue the cycle of work and leisure, but with increasing time spent on the job and decreasing time on the street; many discouraged workers will be drawn into the labor force on a part-time basis; peripheral workers will find that they can get the full-time, well-paid job they wanted but could not otherwise find. Certainly there is a minority that will still choose not to work, but the majority whose condition can be improved should not be denied a legitimate chance because a visible and vocal few are alienated from work.

Clearly, however, work has its alternatives. Unless adequate and attractive opportunities are provided for productive activity, other paths will be chosen. One such route is leisure, and much of street life is nothing more than a way of enjoying spare time. It is too often assumed that employable males loitering on street corners are up to no good; yet if they were out on a golf course, no one would raise an eyebrow. Illicit and antisocial activities are closely connected with street life, but for most of those who are loitering, the purpose is likely to be pleasure rather than profitable crime.

The Low Road

Nevertheless, crime has a significant impact in the life of the older teenager in the ghetto. It casts a discernible shadow on the legitimate labor market activities of young men, although its characteristics and rewards are difficult to measure. In all likelihood, however, illicit income for most youths is not as lucrative as full-time employment. Only a minority are sufficiently lucky or skilled in crime to make big money, but they set the style for others. Crime yields uncertain returns, but it demands little effort and allows much freedom to pursue other interests. The crimes committed for income, such as shakedowns and extortions, numbers running, and drug pushing, can be pursued on a leisurely schedule. Few youths in their late teens are hardened criminals, but many find illegitimate pursuits attractive or express their frustrations through asocial behavior.

The choice between legitimate and illegitimate activities might be rational to some extent, since much illicit activity is a result of the paucity of other opportunities. Nevertheless, income differentials alone cannot explain the high crime rates in the ghetto. The absolute and relative incidence of crime among black urban youths has increased despite improvement in their economic situation. In 1960, 13 of every 100,000 whites were arrested for robbery and 69 of every 100,000 blacks; in 1967 the comparable rates were 23 and 369 respectively, with an even greater increase among young blacks. In a recent study in Stamford, Connecticut, it was concluded that if age and poverty factors could be eliminated, blacks would still be three times more likely to commit a crime than whites. In a more conclusive study in Philadelphia, delinquency rates for every age and income bracket were found to be significantly higher for blacks than for whites.[31] Ghetto life and the contacts the youth makes on the street are probably responsible for these differences. Another major factor may be the rising "legitimacy" of crime, to the extent that blacks see it as an expression of civil disobedience. Youths who watched or participated in urban riots, which generally included massive looting, undoubtedly have fewer qualms about criminal activities.

Whatever the reason, the fact that the incidence of crimes and arrests is rising suggests that more youths are becoming involved in crime. Those who become committed criminals usually get their start in the late teens. They are largely school dropouts, the unemployed, and those outside the labor force. But there is a large element of chance in the criminal selection process. A majority of ghetto youths probably commit crimes of one sort or another, but only a minority are arrested more than once and even a smaller number go to jail. In 1960 there were 11,000 blacks aged from fifteen to nineteen, mostly males, in federal and state prisons or reformatories and in local jails and workhouses. The total constituted 1 percent of the population in this age bracket. Among twenty- to twenty-four-year-old blacks, there were 240,000 in such institutions, or 2 percent of the population.[32] Many more youths pass through these institutions, since there is a 100 percent turnover every year in federal and state prisons and many youthful offenders serve short sentences. In 1966 there were 4.6 juveniles and 1.6 adults on parole or probation for every prisoner.[33] Nonetheless, this evidence indicates that only a small minority of ghetto youths are identified and punished as criminals.

Once a youth has entered prison, however, the chances are high that he will develop into a full-time criminal. A study of prisoners released in 1963 showed that nearly 75 percent of those under twenty and 70 percent of those between twenty and twenty-four were rearrested within six years.[34] Some of those going to prison are already committed to crime; many others learn the tricks of the trade while there, so that crime becomes more productive and alluring. But many are forced into a life of crime because they have no other opportunities. One survey in 1964 found, for example, that 36 percent of juvenile offenders under twenty, and 18 percent of those from twenty to twenty-four were unemployed—extremely high rates, since the sample included white as well as black youths.[35] Employers are reluctant to hire former prisoners, while the correctional institutions provide all too few counseling, rehabilitative, and manpower services to enhance their employability. As things now stand, those who are arrested and sent to prison are usually destined for a life of crime.

SETTLING DOWN

Adopting Adult Employment Patterns

The majority of young males who remain in the civilian noninstitutional population settle down in their early twenties and become stable labor force participants. For nonwhite males aged twenty and twenty-one in the six large city slums sampled in fiscal 1969, an average of 83 percent were labor force participants, 8 percent were in school, and 2 percent were not in the labor force because of ill health, leaving only 7 percent out of the labor force for other reasons. An important factor in this settling-down process is marriage, which creates a demand for steady income and legitimate activities. In the SMSA's with a population of 250,000 or more in 1969, less than 3 percent of nonwhite males aged sixteen to nineteen were married, but the proportion among those twenty to twenty-four was 44 percent. Of these married men, 94 percent were in the work force.

Combined with this push of greater responsibility is the pull of more attractive opportunities. Perhaps the most significant employment development in the early twenties is a massive shift in occupations and industries (Table 5). There is a noticeable shift from service to blue-collar work and an apparent slight occupational upgrading into the craftsman, professional, and technical groupings. Industrially, employment declines slightly in government and the service sector and quite sharply in the wholesale and retail trades. There is a correspondingly large increase in the number employed in manufacturing. The patterns of industrial change are not significantly different for whites throughout these SMSA's, though a much higher percentage goes to retail and wholesale trade and a slightly lower percentage to manufacturing. Occupationally, however, the improvements at this juncture are far more significant for whites. White males in white-collar occupations rise from 25 percent at the sixteen-through nineteen-year level to 43 percent in the next five-year age group, with professionals, technical workers, and managers increasing from 4.5 percent to 24 percent of the total. Service workers and laborers decline from 41 to 15 percent. Comparing these gains for whites with those for ghetto youths in Table 5, it is clear that many more blacks are trapped in secondary employment.

Mobility and Improvement

These occupational and industrial shifts reflect only the net results of extensive job changes that occur within and among firms as youths are establishing their permanent patterns and directions of work. Nonwhite males in urban areas have the highest rates of

TABLE 5

Employment Patterns of Nonwhites in Poverty Neighborhoods of SMSA's with Population of 250,000 and Over, 1969

	16-19	20-24
Occupational Distribution		
White collar	22.5	22.6
Professional and technical	3.0	4.4
Managers	0.4	1.7
Clerical	16.2	15.1
Sales	2.9	1.4
Blue collar	55.3	66.0
Craftsmen	5.3	10.6
Operatives	28.8	34.5
Laborers	21.2	20.9
Service workers	20.7	11.3
Farm	1.5	.2
Industrial Distribution		
Wage and salary	99.6	99.2
Private	83.2	85.6
Agriculture	1.8	.3
Mining	.0	.4
Construction	4.6	7.2
Manufacturing	24.3	43.1
Durable	14.7	29.2
Nondurable	9.6	13.9
Transportation and utilities	4.1	7.4
Wholesale and retail	31.2	5.0
Finance and real estate	2.9	2.7
Service	14.3	9.6
Business	4.8	3.0
Household	1.2	.0
Personal	2.6	2.7
Other	.0	.0
Government	16.5	13.6
Self-employed	.4	.8

Source: U.S. Department of Labor, Bureau of Labor Statistics, Current Population Survey, "Poverty-Non-Poverty Tracts" (unpublished tabulations).

movement between employers and occupations of any age-sex cohort in the population. A national survey of fifteen- to twenty-year-old blacks in 1967 showed that 68 percent of blue-collar workers and 83 percent of those in the service sector had changed employers during the previous year, whereas only about 50 percent of the white youths in the same age bracket had done so. Job-hopping declines sharply as the workers mature, and only 38 percent of nonwhite twenty- to twenty-four-year-olds changed employers between 1966 and 1967. Though the higher rate of employer change among black males results partly from the high separation rates, both voluntary and involuntary, common to the unattractive and low-paying jobs in which they are concentrated, such changes are also a way of increasing satisfaction. For nonwhites from twenty-one to twenty-five years of age, 56 percent of those who changed employers liked their work in 1967 more than they did in 1966, compared with 36 percent of those who stayed with the same employer.[36]

There are also a large number of intrafirm shifts in jobs. For instance, 17 percent of black men aged from twenty to twenty-four made an occupational change between 1966 and 1967 within a firm. Those who make intrafirm occupational changes are usually better off. The median gain in pay rate was 33 percent for job changers, compared with 14 percent for those remaining in the same occupation. Blacks are slightly less likely to make intrafirm changes, but the percentage moving laterally or upward is exactly the same as that of white youths. The differentials in pay and occupational distribution that persist despite these changes suggest that blacks occupy a different track within a firm, so that they begin at a lower plateau and move upward in smaller steps.[37]

Though they are more likely to shift jobs, black youths are less mobile geographically. Only 6 percent of nonwhite males aged from fifteen to twenty-five who were not drafted moved across county lines between 1966 and 1967, compared with 11 percent of whites.[38] For those growing up in the ghetto, there is even less chance of moving. Housing opportunities in the suburbs being what they are, more black youths commute (rather than relocate) to suburban jobs as they get older. The six-city slum survey showed that although only a minority of ghetto youths holds jobs in the suburbs, the proportion is noticeably higher for twenty- to twenty-four-year-old nonwhites than for those aged from sixteen to nineteen, and there is a corresponding decline in the proportion working in the inner city (Table 6). It is interesting to note that a higher percentage of nonwhite than white twenty- to twenty-four-year-olds living in the slums hold suburban jobs. This pattern suggests that they may be losing out in competition for central city employment or that they are more motivated to seek attractive suburban jobs.

As a result of these many changes in the early twenties, the nonwhite youth generally improves his position, both absolutely and relatively: unemployment rates fall; labor force participation rates rise; hourly wages increase; and the differences in labor market behavior between whites and nonwhites decline. Between 1966 and 1967, the median wage range for twenty-one- to twenty-five-year-old whites who shifted occupations rose by 21 percent while the gain for nonwhites was 33 percent.[39] The median earnings of black male family heads under the age of twenty-five rose by 94 percent between 1960 and 1970, a greater increase than for any other

TABLE 6

Usual Place of Work*

| | Male Slum Area Residents | | | |
	Nonwhite 16-19	Nonwhite 20-24	White 16-19	White 20-24
Within City Limits	88%	78%	84%	83%
Inner City	31	22	29	23
Remainder of City	57	56	55	60
Outside City Limits	12	22	16	17

*Those with same address each day.

Source: U.S. Department of Labor, Bureau of Labor Statistics, Urban Employment Survey (unpublished).

nonwhite or white age group. It is fairly clear, then, that opportunities have been expanding for committed nonwhite workers in their early twenties, and individuals can improve their position substantially.

Nevertheless, earnings for blacks are still substantially less than for whites, even among those in similar occupations. Black craftsmen and operatives who were under the age of twenty-five and family heads in 1970 had 1969 median earnings of $5,229, compared with $6,178 for whites.[40] The unemployment rate for black ghetto teenagers in the large SMSA's was 2.1 times that for all teenage metropolitan whites in 1970; for twenty- to twenty-four-year-old blacks, the rate was still 1.8 times as high.[41] But the problem of underemployment probably intensifies in the early twenties as committed black workers are forced into jobs that pay low wages and that do not utilize or develop their abilities. The qualitative differentials between white and nonwhite employment probably increase in significance, though these aspects are difficult to measure.

The Credentials Gap

A major reason for the continuing disparity between nonwhite and white employment patterns is that the black youth is more likely to be poorly prepared for and ill adjusted to the world of work. When he is ready to settle down and form more stable job attachments, he is often unqualified for many types of employment. But individual handicaps do not account for all of his problems.

Black youths' substantial gains in educational attainment over the past decade have not brought commensurate improvements in their labor market status. Additional years of education have not raised the employment and earnings of nonwhites as much as they have for whites. And most young black males have more education than they need for jobs they get. Chart 4 shows that the number of nonwhites completing high school has increased at a faster rate than the number working in occupations that normally require a diploma; that nonwhite dropouts who want to work have about the same chance as nonwhite graduates of finding a job, though there is a marked difference between white graduates and white dropouts; and

CHART 4.   RELATIVE BENEFITS OF EDUCATION TO WHITE AND NONWHITE MALES

A. EDUCATION AND OCCUPATION, NONWHITE MALES 16 AND OVER

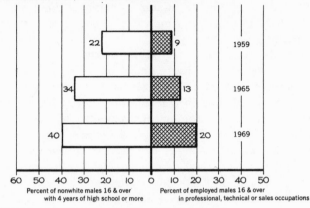

Percent of nonwhite males 16 & over
with 4 years of high school or more

Percent of employed males 16 & over
in professional, technical or sales occupations

SOURCE: U.S. Department of Labor, *Manpower Report of the President, 1970.*

B. EDUCATION AND UNEMPLOYMENT, 1969, FOR 16–21-YEAR-OLD MALES

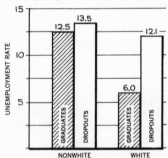

SOURCE: U.S. Department of Labor, Bureau of Labor Statistics,
"Employment of High School Graduates and Dropouts, 1969."

C. PERCENT 25–44-YEAR-OLD MALES EARNING LESS THAN $3,000, BY RACE, 1969

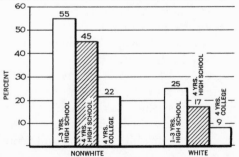

SOURCE: U.S. Department of Labor, Bureau of Labor Statistics.

70

that while education is associated with higher earnings for nonwhites, the proportionate gains are not as great as they are for whites who get a high school diploma.

These data deal with all nonwhites, and for those located in central city slums the gains from increased education are even less. A study focusing on these areas showed that while education was significantly correlated with occupational status, it had only a nominal relationship to higher wages and a statistically insignificant correlation with reduced unemployment.[42] Chart 5 was calculated from a regression model fitted to data for the central city poverty areas of the twelve largest SMSA's. The estimates of earnings, unemployment, and education are adjusted for differences in age, sex, city of residence, and industry for nearly 12,000 individuals in the sample. Quite clearly, nonwhites benefit from increased education in terms of earnings, but their gains are far less than those of white residents of slum areas. Education appears to be of little benefit to nonwhites in reducing the incidence of unemployment. Thus, increased education—especially a college degree—helps to improve employment conditions for ghetto blacks, but it does not come close to reducing interracial differentials, since whites benefit so much more than nonwhites.

To a large extent, then, the problem of black youths as they settle down is that their "credentials" are not respected. A high school diploma does not provide the same access that it does for whites. Employers justify their double standard by the valid assertion that on the average the black youth is not as well educated as the white, even if both come from the ghetto. But blanket exclusions bar black youths whose educational achievements match those of whites, and they exclude many more who could do the work, whatever their success in school. There is mounting evidence that employers overestimate the academic skills needed on the job, that those who are overeducated are often dissatisfied with their work, and that many who are excluded could, if given a chance, be more stable and productive employees.[43] There is some justification for giving less credence to a black's high school diploma if it reflects real differences in achievement, if alternative means to test ability are not available, and if educational differences are directly related to differences in productivity. The fact is that such rational criteria are not necessarily controlling, and black youths are barred from work

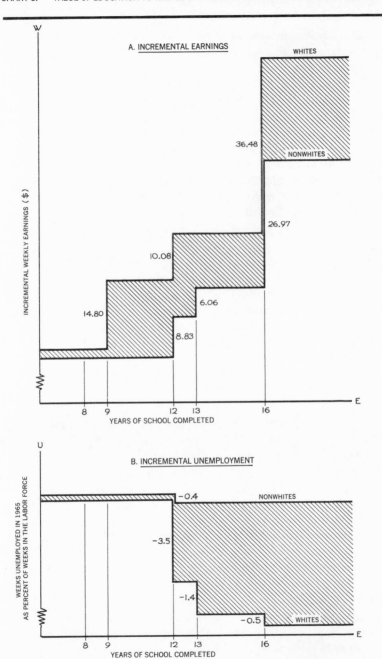

SOURCE: Bennett Harrison, "Education, Training, and the Urban Ghetto," Ph.D. diss., University of Pennsylvania, 1970.

that would fully utilize and develop their abilities. The cancerous effects of discrimination have been well documented, and despite the advancements made in the 1960's racial prejudice continues to inflict its toll on blacks.

NOTES

1. U.S. Department of Commerce, Bureau of the Census, *Trends in Social and Economic Conditions in Metropolitan and Nonmetropolitan Areas*, Current Population Reports, series P-23, no. 33 (Washington, D.C.: Government Printing Office, September 1970), pp. 16-29.

2. *Ibid.*, pp. 25, 73-74.

3. Herbert Parnes *et al., Career Thresholds*, vol. 1, Manpower Research Monograph no. 16, Manpower Administration, U.S. Department of Labor (Washington, D.C.: Government Printing Office, 1970), pp. 178-83.

4. Thorsten Sellin and Marvin E. Wolfgang, "The Extent and Character of Delinquency in an Age Cohort" (Philadelphia: University of Pennsylvania, 1969; mimeographed); Alfred Blumstein, "Systems Analysis and the Criminal Justice System," *Annals of the American Academy of Political and Social Science*, November 1967, pp. 92-100.

5. U.S. Department of Justice, Federal Bureau of Investigation, *Crime in the United States* (Washington, D.C.: Government Printing Office, August 1970), pp. 122-25.

6. Fred P. Graham, "Black Crime: The Lawless Image," *Harper's*, September 1970, pp. 64-71.

7. James P. Coleman, *Equality of Education Opportunity* (Washington, D.C.: Government Printing Office, 1966), p. 275.

8. Federal Bureau of Investigation, *Crime*, pp. 122-23.

9. Frederick Zeller *et al.*, *Career Thresholds*, vol. 2 (Columbus, Ohio: Center for Human Resource Research, The Ohio State University, 1970), p. 69.

10. Parnes *et al*, *Career Thresholds*, vol. 1, pp. 26, 167.

11. *Ibid.*, p. 51.

12. Zeller *et al.*, *Career Thresholds*, vol. 2, pp. 5-7.

13. William Bowen and Aldrich Finegan, *The Economics of Labor Force Participation* (Princeton, N.J.: Princeton University Press, 1969), p. 449.

14. Anne M. Young, "Employment of School-Age Youth," *Monthly Labor Review*, September 1970, pp. 4-11.

15. *Ibid.*, p. 7.

16. Bennett Harrison, "Education, Training, and the Urban Ghetto," Ph.D. diss., University of Pennsylvania, 1970.

17. Parnes *et al.*, *Career Thresholds*, vol. 1, p. 22.

18. Coleman, *Equality*, p. 275.

19. Zeller *et al.*, *Career Thresholds*, vol. 2, p. 7.

20. U.S. Department of Commerce, Bureau of the Census, *The Social and Economic Status of Negroes in the United States, 1969*, Current Population Reports, series P-23, no. 29 (Washington, D.C.: Government Printing Office, 1970), p. 87.

21. U.S. Department of the Army, Office of the Surgeon General, "Supplement to Health of the Army" (Washington, D.C., June 1969; mimeographed).

22. The President's Task Force on Manpower Conservation, *One-Third of a Nation* (Washington, D.C.: Government Printing Office, 1964).

23. Elizabeth Waldman, "Vietnam War Veterans—Transition to Civilian Life," *Monthly Labor Review*, November 1970, p. 23.

24. Jack Ladinsky, "A Survey of Socially and Economically Disadvantaged Vietnam Era Veterans" (Washington, D.C.: Bureau of the Budget, November 1969; mimeographed), app. A.

25. Charles Killingsworth, "Rising Unemployment: A 'Transitional' Problem?" *Manpower Development and Training Legislation, 1970*, Hearings before the Senate Subcommittee on Employment, Manpower and Poverty, 91st Cong., 1st and 2nd Sess., March 25, 1970, pp. 1256-57.

26. Alice H. Kidder, "Interracial Comparisons of Labor Market Behavior," Ph.D. diss., Massachusetts Institute of Technology, August 1967.

27. Parnes *et al.*, *Career Thresholds*, vol. 1, p. 12.

28. Edwin Harwood, "A Tale of Two Ghettos," *The Public Interest*, fall 1969, pp. 78-87.

29. U.S. Department of Labor, *Youth Unemployment and Minimum Wages*, Bulletin 1657 (Washington, D.C.: Government Printing Office, 1970), pp. 99-103.

30. Elliot Liebow, *Tally's Corner* (Boston: Little, Brown & Co., 1967).

31. Graham, "Black Crime," pp. 64-71.

32. U.S. Department of Commerce, Bureau of the Census, *Statistical Abstract of the United States: 1970* (Washington, D.C.: 1970), p. 156.

33. Sylvia G. McCollum, "Education and Training of Youthful Offenders," *The Transition From School to Work* (Princeton, N.J.: Princeton University Press, 1968), p. 108.

34. Federal Bureau of Investigation, *Crime*, p. 39.

35. George A. Pownall, "Employment Problems of Released Prisoners," preliminary report (Washington, D.C.: Office of Manpower Policy, Evaluation and Research, U.S. Department of Labor, 1968; mimeographed), p. 32.

36. Zeller *et al., Career Thresholds*, vol. 2, pp. 28, 38.

37. *Ibid.*, pp. 45, 48.

38. *Ibid.*, p. 49.

39. *Ibid.*, p. 47.

40. U.S. Department of Commerce, Bureau of the Census, *Occupation and Earnings of Family Heads in 1969, 1965, and 1959*, Current Population Reports, series P-60, no. 73 (Washington, D.C.: Government Printing Office, September 30, 1970), pp. 17, 18.

41. U.S. Department of Labor, Bureau of Labor Statistics, Current Population Survey, "Poverty-Non-Poverty Tracts" (unpublished tabulations, 1970).

42. Harrison, "Education, Training."

43. Ivar Berg, *Education and Jobs* (New York: Praeger, 1970).

From the day she is born, the black female faces the same
obstacles her brother faces—unstable family, poverty, poor schools,
discrimination, and detrimental peer-group influences. And these
obstacles have a similar effect: by the time she reaches working age,
the black girl in the ghetto is often unable to compete in the labor
market with others from more affluent circumstances. But these
factors interact to retard her development in different ways than
they do for a black man, and the impact is far more inimical in
limiting her adjustment to the world of work. Where street life,
crime, and the draft figure prominently in the life of the young male,
family responsibilities, unwanted children, and welfare are important
factors for the young woman. All too many black girls follow a
pattern of moving from school and full-time household responsibilities in the parents' home to motherhood (with or without marriage)
and dependency in lieu of work. The labor market offers few
options, and its inadequacies compound the handicaps of the black
girl's background. Thus her employment problems are even more
severe than those of the ghetto male.

ADJUSTMENT IN THE SCHOOL AND HOME

By the time she reaches her early teens, the black girl is more
mature in many ways than the average white girl. Coming from a

lower-income family or a broken home where the mother must work, or from a household with a large brood of children needing care, she must assume many responsibilities. Usually she has numerous household chores after school and during the summers; school therefore becomes an attractive alternative to drudgery in the home, offering the chance to be with friends and to become involved with less demanding work. Apparently for this reason, the black girl is more likely than the white to express satisfaction with her academic experience. One survey showed that 61 percent of fourteen- to seventeen-year-old blacks "liked school very much," compared with 53 percent of whites. Nonetheless, more blacks than whites drop out; 7 percent of nonwhite fourteen- and fifteen-year-old girls are out of school, compared with only 2 percent of white girls and just 5 percent of nonwhite males of this age. The reason is obvious: more than half of the blacks who are not enrolled are married or have illegitimate children.[1]

With school attendance and responsibilities in the home, only one of every three black girls is likely to look for work before her sixteenth birthday. Work experience and search for jobs is highly seasonal at this early age, in 1970 ranging from 23 percent of all fourteen- and fifteen-year-olds in July to 6 percent in November. White girls this age are much more likely to work while in school, and their unemployment rates are substantially lower than those of blacks.[2]

The sixteenth year is a critical one for females as well as for males because school attendance requirements generally end and child labor laws become less restrictive. The proportion of nonwhite girls who are not enrolled in school jumps from 7 percent for fourteen- and fifteen-year-olds to 17.5 percent for those aged sixteen and seventeen; among whites it rises to only 9.3 percent.[3] The difference is largely explained by the much larger proportion of nonwhite girls who drop out of school to assume the responsibilities of motherhood.

The significance of early childbearing is indicated in Chart 6. Only 1 percent of sixteen- and seventeen-year-old white girls who are not married have children, compared with 10 percent of blacks. Since the children of these girls require care, only a small proportion are able or willing to work, and even fewer can find jobs. Of out-of-school black girls aged sixteen and seventeen, 38 percent were

CHART 6. MARITAL AND FAMILY STATUS OF 14- TO 24-YEAR-OLD FEMALES BY RACE, 1968

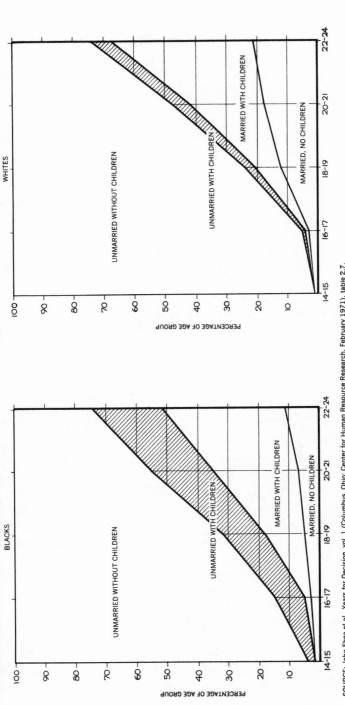

SOURCE: John Shea et al., Years for Decision, vol. 1 (Columbus, Ohio: Center for Human Resource Research, February 1971), table 2.7.

in the labor force in October 1969, compared with 47 percent for whites. Nearly 50 percent of these black girls were unemployed, twice the rate among whites.[4]

But the great majority of sixteen- and seventeen-year-old black girls, 90 percent, are in school. Among fourteen- to seventeen-year-old students, nonwhite girls have greater educational aspirations than whites. One survey showed that 54 percent wanted a college education, compared with 48 percent of whites and that of these, nearly 80 percent expected to attend for two years or more despite the difficulties they knew they would encounter.[5] Of course, these aspirations and expectations are unrealistic in view of the fact that less than 25 percent of those aged from twenty-two to twenty-four had completed one year of college or more.[6] They are especially unrealistic in light of nonwhite youths' underachievement and underattainment. Despite their aspirations and their satisfaction with school, black girls are several grades behind their white peers, according to achievement scales.[7] They are also often behind in attainment, as suggested by the estimate that 14 percent of black girls in the ninth through eleventh grades are over seventeen, compared with only 5 percent of whites.[8]

At the ages of sixteen and seventeen students begin to seek part-time and summer work. Blacks are apparently less likely to look for or find jobs during school but are more likely to seek employment in the summer. Among nonwhite students, the labor force participation rate in October 1969 was 22.1 percent, 33 percent being unemployed; the comparable rates among whites were 35.2 percent in the labor force and 12.1 percent unemployed.[9] Yet 58 percent of black female students of this age had held jobs at one time or another, compared with 57 percent of whites, suggesting that nonwhite girls are more likely to seek and find employment during the school holidays.[10]

One reason for the lower labor force participation rate among black girls may be that they want to concentrate on their school studies. But it is more likely that they are discouraged by the difficulty of finding a job. Whichever is the case, those who do seek employment are more likely than whites to be driven by economic necessity. The labor force participation rate for black sixteen- and seventeen-year-old girls from families with one working parent employed less than 2,000 hours annually was 45 percent, compared with 25 percent when the parents worked 2,000 hours or more. The exact opposite was the case for whites, where there was a higher rate of participation in families whose heads worked more steadily.[11] Recognizing present and future responsibilities, black girls are more acclimated to the idea of work. Nearly 50 percent of the black girls enrolled in the ninth, tenth, and eleventh grades plan to be working when they reach the age of thirty-five; only 25 percent of white girls anticipate being employed at that age. When asked the most important feature of a job, 21 percent of blacks believed good wages were more important than liking the work, compared with 7 percent of whites. Black girls seem to be more concerned about income and more realistic about their future prospects.[12]

WOMANHOOD, WORK, AND WELFARE

At the ages of eighteen and nineteen, the black girls who are still in school usually end their enrollment by either graduating or dropping out. Few go on to college; only 14 percent of all eighteen- and nineteen-year-old black women were attending in March 1970, though more may enter later.[13] More than 60 percent of the black girls are out of school at this age.

Among those women who are not enrolled, employment patterns differ between those with children and those without. The pattern is as expected: blacks who have children, whether or not they are married, work fewer weeks on the average and have a lower labor force participation rate than do those without children; unmarried women without children are more likely to work than any other group (Table 7).

In comparing the aggregate labor force experience of white and nonwhite girls, differing marital and parental patterns are important. Unmarried women with children have the lowest participation rates for both whites and blacks, but since they constitute 16 percent of black eighteen- and nineteen-year-olds and only 4 percent of whites in this group, the aggregate rates for nonwhites are lower. Unemployment rates are also affected, but the direction of the impact is not as clear. If each of the four groups of blacks shown in Table 7 were represented in the out-of-school population in the same

TABLE 7

**Employment Status of 18- and 19-Year-Old Women
by Marital and Family Status, 1969**

	Labor Force Participation Rate		Unemployment Rate	
	Black	White	Black	White
Married, No Children	56.0	64.5	44.4	20.7
Married, With Children	56.1	39.5	27.3	33.7
Unmarried, No Children	71.9	76.0	17.8	8.3
Unmarried, With Children	47.8	33.0	10.5	3.8
Average	64.2	66.3	21.1	13.0

Source: John Shea *et al., Years for Decision*, vol. I (Columbus, Ohio: Center for Human Resource Research, February 1971), Table 5.1.

proportion as is found among whites, the average rate of unemployment would still be higher for blacks. Improvements in marital and family status would undoubtedly leave the average black girl in a better economic position since she would not have as many responsibilities, but such improvements would probably have only a limited impact upon reducing unemployment rates among older teenagers.

An important development among black women in the late teens and early twenties is an increased reliance on welfare. The proportion of ummarried black women with children jumps markedly at the ages of twenty and twenty-one. Perhaps those who abstained or practiced care in their late teens find motherhood an acceptable alternative to the discouraging prospects in the employment market. Many single women who had a child earlier have a second or third at this age, and with more mouths to feed they may have no alternative to welfare. There is also an increase in the number of broken homes. According to the six-city slum survey, 15 percent of sixteen- to nineteen-year-old women are married, but the spouse is absent in 25 percent of these cases. Among twenty- to twenty-four-year-olds, the proportion who are married rises to 45 percent, but the proportion without a husband present rises to 40 percent. While many black wives have no children or are supported by their husbands, and while many of these women can support themselves (better, perhaps, than when the husband is home), a substantial number are unable to maintain economic independence and to cope with child care responsibilities. The result is an increasing dependency on welfare, even though proportionately more nonwhite women aged from twenty-two to twenty-four are in the labor force than whites. In 1969, there were 35,300 black mothers under twenty receiving AFDC, 116,900 between twenty and twenty-four, and 121,800 between twenty-five and twenty-nine.[14]

The availability of child-care facilities is an important factor determining whether a woman with children will work or will rely solely on welfare. Almost 80 percent of employed young black mothers reported a need to find regular child-care arrangements. Of those who made arrangements, 60 percent had relatives care for their children (as compared with only 50 percent of white women in the same position), and only 20 percent placed them in school or child-care centers. The median cost to black mothers who had to pay for child care was $3.21 per day at home and $2.56 per day for group care.[15] Obviously, if relatives are not around to help out, work can be an expensive proposition. Added to child-care costs are travel expenses of about 60 to 70 cents per day and perhaps $1 or $2 for other work-related expenses. For many mothers, this rules out most low-paying work, and especially part-time work, as simply uneconomical. Welfare becomes the more attractive alternative.

In their late teens and early twenties, females who are not shackled by family responsibilities and dependency begin to form more permanent attachments to work, meanwhile going through major shifts in occupational and industrial patterns of employment. These changes are not so drastic as they are for males but have the same result of leaving nonwhites further behind whites. White

women in their early twenties working in urban areas improve
their occupational status; black women do not (Table 8). The
proportion of black women in service work declines somewhat
while that of black women in blue-collar work increases. For
urban whites, service work declines precipitously as white-collar
work expands. Blue-collar jobs remain much less important to
whites than nonwhites.

These occupational changes are reflected in the changing
patterns of employment by industry. Nonwhite women move
increasingly into manufacturing, and the proportion employed in
the government sector declines. Whites, on the other hand,
increase their share in manufacturing and in government, with a
decline in retail and service work.

Once these occupational and industrial shifts of the early
twenties have taken place, women's employment patterns remain
fairly stable. But the interracial differences in labor force
participation rates change radically as black women assume
greater responsibilities as breadwinners. The differentials in
unemployment fluctuate widely with age but remain consistently
higher for black women (Table 9).

A much larger proportion of nonwhite women are also
trapped in low-paying, dead end jobs. For instance, only 10
percent of the unmarried whites with no children who were
employed in February 1968 earned less than $1.50 per hour (ten
cents below the federal minimum wage), compared with 23
percent of blacks. Young black women apparently tend to
concentrate in industries and occupations not covered by the
federal minimum wage legislation.[16]

The Department of Labor six-city slum area study showed
that young females from urban poverty areas, both black and
white, tend to work in central cities and that their mobility to jobs in
the suburbs is restricted. Only 10 percent of twenty- to
twenty-four-year-old women living in urban slums worked in
suburban jobs. Interestingly, while 32 percent of employed whites
from poverty areas held jobs in the inner city, only 22 percent of the
nonwhites worked there. It is apparent that black women, like black
males, are unable to get the better jobs that are close to them, losing
out to whites.

TABLE 8

Occupational and Industrial Distribution of Women Aged 16-24
in SMSA's with a Population Over 250,000, 1969

	White Women Aged		Nonwhites in Poverty Neighborhoods Aged	
	16-19	20-24	16-19	20-24
Occupational Distribution				
White-Collar	64.0%	79.4%	60.0%	56.1%
Professional and technical	4.1	18.0	1.4	6.9
Managers	.6	2.1	.0	.8
Clerical	47.2	54.8	54.0	45.3
Sales	12.1	4.5	4.5	3.0
Blue-Collar	8.1	8.8	11.8	22.9
Craftsmen	.4	.6	.4	.5
Operatives	6.9	8.0	10.0	20.6
Laborers	.8	.3	1.4	.8
Service	27.6	11.7	27.7	20.5
Farm	.3	.1	.5	.5
Industrial Distribution				
Wage and Salary	99.0%	98.8%	99.8%	99.2%
Private	90.8	81.7	74.7	78.4
Agriculture	.3	.3	.5	.6
Mining	.1	.2	.0	.1
Construction	.4	.7	.2	.2
Manufacturing	12.3	18.7	11.5	20.9
Durable	5.7	10.6	6.2	13.2
Nondurable	6.6	8.2	5.4	7.7
Transportation and Utilities	5.0	7.0	9.9	5.6
Wholesale and Retail	32.0	15.8	18.0	16.2
Finance and Real Estate	9.6	12.6	6.4	10.1
Service	31.0	26.3	28.1	24.8
Business	2.7	3.9	2.5	1.6
Household	10.9	1.2	4.8	2.4
Personal	4.0	3.9	3.3	4.9
Other	13.4	14.3	17.5	15.9
Government	8.1	17.1	25.1	20.8
Self-Employed	.6	1.0	.3	.6
Unpaid Family	.4	.2	.0	.2

Source: U.S. Department of Labor, Bureau of Labor Statistics, Current
Population Survey, "Poverty-Non-Poverty Tracts" (unpublished tabulations).

TABLE 9

**Employment Experience of Females Aged 16 to 24,
October 1969**

Age	Labor Force Participation Rate			Unemployment Rate		
	Nonwhites	Whites	NW/W	Nonwhites	Whites	NW/W
16-17	24.4	36.6	.67	35.7	14.5	2.46
18-19	49.0	54.5	.90	30.1	8.9	3.38
20-21	54.8	58.5	.94	11.2	7.7	1.45
22-24	66.4	55.0	1.21	11.6	4.8	2.41

Source: Anne M. Young, "Employment of School Age Youth, October 1969," *Special Labor Force Report No. 124*, Bureau of Labor Statistics, September 1970, Table A-11.

PERSONAL SHORTCOMINGS AND
LABOR MARKET DEFICIENCIES

For policy purposes it is important to know whether the problems of black women, which are so much greater than those of white women, result from educational deficiencies or from greater fecundity and other behavioral patterns or whether they are external and can be alleviated, if not eliminated, through improvements in the labor market mechanisms.

The Value of Education

Differences in educational achievement account for much of the interracial differentials in earnings. The evidence indicates, however, that additional schooling will hardly eliminate existing gaps because black women, like black men, benefit less from educational attainment than whites (Chart 7). Since white high school dropouts have experienced lower unemployment rates than black graduates, barring other changes, progress in reducing the number of dropouts will not significantly close the employment gap between blacks and whites. Furthermore, penetration into white-collar jobs has barely kept pace with the growth in the proportion of high school graduates. Unless the rate of penetration greatly exceeds educational gains, the underrepresentation of black women in the more attractive jobs in our economy will continue and the payoff on education will not be large. Other data show that the average hourly wage differentials between whites and blacks are significant at all levels of educational attainment and in all but the white-collar occupations.

If black females are to earn as much as whites, or more, they must get into white-collar jobs.[17]

Aside from discrimination, the barrier to finding white-collar jobs may be the lack of specific skills as much as the lack of general education. Nonwhite females are less likely than whites to have learned typing and shorthand in high school. Only 25 percent of black women, compared with more than 40 percent of white women, learned both. The value of clerical skills is shown by the fact that among eighteen- to twenty-four-year-olds who were not enrolled in school, blacks with typing and shorthand had an unemployment rate of 7.7 percent in February 1968, compared with 19.6 percent for those with only typing and 23.2 percent for those with neither.[18] Provisions for such training would certainly have a favorable impact on helping blacks to penetrate white-collar jobs where unemployment rates are lower and wages higher.

The Causes and Costs of Fecundity

Another factor that contributes to the problems of black women is their greater fecundity. Childbearing itself restricts work, and once born, a child requires attention at home. As indicated earlier, 63 percent of the twenty- to twenty-four-year-old black women have children, compared with 54 percent of whites, and

CHART 7. BENEFITS OF EDUCATION TO NONWHITE FEMALES, OCTOBER 1969

A. UNEMPLOYMENT RATE OF 16- TO 21-YEAR-OLD FEMALES

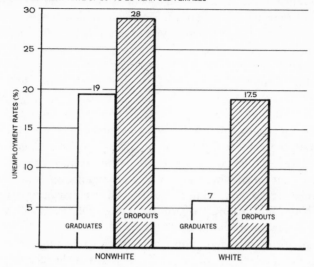

SOURCE: U.S. Department of Labor, Bureau of Labor Statistics,
"Employment of High School Graduates and Dropouts, 1969."

B. EDUCATION AND OCCUPATION OF NONWHITE FEMALES 16 AND OVER

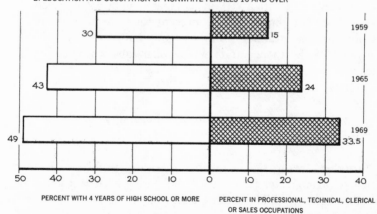

PERCENT WITH 4 YEARS OF HIGH SCHOOL OR MORE   PERCENT IN PROFESSIONAL, TECHNICAL, CLERICAL
                                                            OR SALES OCCUPATIONS

SOURCE: U.S. Department of Labor, Manpower Report of the President, 1970.

black women who have children are likely to bear more than one child. While the increased use of contraceptive techniques has reduced childbearing over the past decade and the legalizing of abortion is likely to reduce the number of unwanted children further, the decrease has been least apparent among young nonwhites. The cumulative number of children born to twenty-through twenty-four-year-old blacks fell from 1.3 in 1960 to 1.0 in 1969; but the decline from 1.0 to 0.6 for whites was significantly larger. Illegitimacy rates for nonwhite women in their early twenties have fallen, but those for fifteen- to nineteen-year-olds have increased, and both are much higher than for whites (Table 10). Persons from low-income families are more often ignorant of, or lack access to, methods of contraception or abortion, with the result that unwanted and unplanned pregnancies are more numerous than among more affluent groups.

It is also probable that to some unmarried young women pregnancy may not be unwelcome. When responsibilities are burdensome in their parents' home, or when school work is difficult

TABLE 10

Estimated Illegitimacy Rates by Age of Mother, Selected Years 1950-67

| Age group | (Rates per 1,000 Unmarried Women) | | | |
	1950	1960	1965	1967
Nonwhite				
15-19	68.5	76.5	75.8	80.2
20-24	105.4	166.5	152.6	128.2
White				
15-19	5.1	6.6	7.9	9.0
20-24	10.0	18.2	22.1	23.1

Source: *The Social and Economic Status of Negroes in the United States, 1969.*

or unattractive, the young woman may find that motherhood is an easier road to independence than work. In mid-1971 a mother with one child on public assistance received $228 monthly in Chicago, $219 in New York, and $181 in Detroit. Cash payments are often supplemented by food stamps, public housing, and health care. The total real income on welfare may not seem much, but the median hourly wage of sixteen- to nineteen-year-old poverty area girls was only $1.68 in Chicago and Detroit and $2.00 in New York in 1969.[19] Since 25 percent of those looking for work could not find employment and 40 percent with jobs worked less than thirty-five hours per week, the average young black woman could probably earn no more than $2,500 per year. On welfare in Detroit, she could get $2,200 in cash payments and ample time to supplement her income. While it is doubtful that having second and third children has an economic basis, the first child can be a rational decision for the young woman living in a state with liberal welfare levels, especially if she faces no social opprobrium and if she can thereby escape unpleasant circumstances in her parents' home.

Nonetheless, most children born to young black girls out of wedlock are probably unwanted. The obvious solution is to increase the awareness and use of contraceptives or the access to abortion if other preventive measures fail. Schools, churches, and homes might teach more about contraceptive techniques, combining this education with free distribution of contraceptives and medical assistance to all who desire them, regardless of age or marital status.

Though the reduction of birth rates among young blacks could have many favorable effects, it would not eliminate the interracial employment differentials. Black women are more likely to be unemployed than white women no matter what their family status and educational level (Table 11). If all else remained the same, unemployment rates for black women would probably grow worse rather than better if more women become labor force participants through the prevention of unwanted children.

The Critical Job Shortage

The employment problems of black girls, perhaps even more than those of males, are a function of inadequate demand. There are

TABLE 11

Incidence of Unemployment in 1967, by Family Status,
Highest Year of School Completed, and Color:
Women 18-24 Years of Age with Work Experience
and Not Enrolled in School

Family Status and Highest Year of School Completed	Total Number with Some Unemployment as Percent of Number in Labor Force in 1967		Weeks of Unemployment as Percent of Weeks in Labor Force in 1967	
	Whites	Blacks	Whites	Blacks
Without children	22.8	37.9	3.9	9.8
Less than 12	30.8	42.4	6.0	15.8
12	22.5	36.5	4.2	8.7
13 or more	21.0	36.6	3.4	7.3
With children	22.8	32.3	6.8	11.9
Less than 12	21.1	33.2	6.0	14.3
12	22.1	31.0	6.7	9.0
13 or more	1.7	21.2	1.8	7.6
Total or average[a]	22.7	35.4	4.6	10.8
Less than 12	26.6	35.9	6.0	15.0
12	22.2	34.9	4.6	8.9
13 or more	21.1	31.9	3.9	7.5

[a]Includes women for whom family status was not ascertained.

Source: Calculated from John Shea *et al., Years of Decision* vol. 1 (Columbus, Ohio: Center for Human Resource Research, February 1971), Table 5.2.

too few jobs for those who want to work, and the openings that are left for black women are the least attractive. Increasing skills and rising levels of labor force participation are not much use when jobs are in short supply.

Women from the ghetto are at the very end of the labor queue. Besides the handicaps of being black, poorly educated, and locked in the ghetto, they face the additional burden of their sex. Too many employers will hire a young black girl only when no other potential employees are available, and even then some may prefer to leave their openings vacant.

Cross-sectional data show that unemployment and labor force participation rates are closely correlated to demand in the local labor market. Black girls need both a low rate of aggregate unemployment and a high level of demand for female labor to improve their position relative to whites (Table 12).

Even when unemployment is low, forced idleness of black girls in the ghetto remains incredibly high. Nearly 20 percent of all eighteen- to twenty-four-year-old black women who wanted jobs could not find work in 1967. And this measure understates the real job shortage. For black females, even more than for males, there is a significant amount of disguised unemployment—would-be workers who have become discouraged and have dropped out of the labor force. As indicated earlier, data for the six-city slum areas showed that almost 50 percent of the nonwhite teenage girls who are not in the labor force say they would seek work if jobs were available. Though these statements are probably exaggerated, there is no doubt that increases in the number of jobs open to nonwhite women would raise the rates of labor force participation and lower the levels of unemployment. Clearly, the *sine qua non* for the employment problems of black girls is to increase the number of available jobs and to achieve sustained tight labor markets that could absorb the labor force dropouts as well as the unemployed.

Special Efforts for Women

More attention clearly needs to be given to the needs of black women. Their problems are of critical dimensions, and it is difficult to understand why they are receiving so little attention. Increasingly, women are entering the labor force for reasons of economic necessity, not as secondary workers. This is especially true of black women. Those who gainsay the massive unemployment and extremely low wages among young black women are ignoring the very marked differences between the marital and family patterns of blacks and whites: 25 percent of black women aged from twenty to twenty-four are unmarried mothers, and in the ghetto, more than 33 percent of those who are married have no spouse present.[20] Even

TABLE 12

Unemployment Rates, by Selected Characteristics of Local Labor Market and Color: Women 18-24 Years of Age in the Labor Force and Not Enrolled in School[a]

Characteristics of Local Labor Market	Whites		Blacks	
	Labor Force Participation	Unemployment	Labor Force Participation	Unemployment
Index of demand for female labor[b]				
High	66.2	9.8	68.0	15.8
Low	56.9	9.7	58.3	20.3
Total or average	61.8	9.8	63.7	17.6
1967 unemployment rate				
Less than 3.1 percent	64.0	7.3	64.0	13.2
3.1-5.0 percent	61.0	10.8	66.5	16.9
5.1 percent or more	60.8	11.0	59.6	21.5
Total or average	61.8	9.8	63.7	17.6

aIncludes only women with work experience.

bThe labor market's industry mix is weighted by the national fraction of each industry's employment represented by women.

Source: John Shea *et al., Years of Decision*, vol. 1 (Columbus, Ohio: Center for Human Resource Research, February 1971), tables 4.8, 4.9.

when the family is stable, the wife may be the prime or major breadwinner. In terms of their family responsibilities, therefore, young black women clearly need jobs as much as or more than men. There is no reason that women should receive less attention in the efforts to solve the employment problems of black youth. Certain strategies will be more effective in dealing with the problems of women. In terms of cost birth control is, of course, extremely effective. Motherhood forces girls to drop out of school and frequently to join the welfare rolls if the father does not assume responsibility for support of the child. Unwanted children, even in stable families, are a financial burden and often preclude work by the mother.

But the real key to helping young women in the labor market is to create jobs. As far as possible, employment opportunities must be opened in the private sector by forcing an end to discrimination and by subsidizing the hiring and training of black girls. Because their chances are limited, women have low wage expectations and are likely to take jobs that young black males would spurn. The problem is to convince employers to forgo their prejudices; and one effective way to overcome discrimination may be through subsidies. But the private sector is unlikely to generate all the jobs needed by black girls, and public employment may be the only alternative to relief. The positions created need not be stigmatized as "work experience" jobs but should serve as stepping stones to permanent positions in the public or private sector.

NOTES

1. John Shea et al., Years for Decision, vol. 1 (Columbus, Ohio: Center for Human Resource Research, The Ohio State University, 1971), tables 2.4, 2.7.

2. Employment and Earnings, August 1970, p. 35, and December 1970, p. 43.

3. Shea et al., Years for Decision, table 2.7.

4. Anne M. Young, "Employment of School Age Youth, October 1969," U.S. Department of Labor, Bureau of Labor Statistics, *Special Labor Force Report 124*, September 1970, table A-11.

5. Shea *et al.*, *Years of Decision*, table 7.1.

6. U.S. Department of Commerce, Bureau of the Census, "Educational Attainment, March 1970," Current Population Reports, series P-20, no. 207, p. 15.

7. James P. Coleman, *Equality of Educational Opportunity* (Washington, D.C.: Government Printing Office, 1966), p. 275.

8. Shea *et al.*, *Years for Decision*, table 2.2.

9. Young, "Employment of School-Age Youth," table A-11.

10. Shea *et al.*, *Years for Decision*, table A-1.

11. *Ibid.*, table 3-2.

12. *Ibid.*, tables 2.16-2.18.

13. Bureau of the Census, "Educational Attainment, March 1970," p. 151.

14. U.S. Department of Health, Education and Welfare, Social and Rehabilitation Service, "Preliminary Report of Findings—1969 AFDC Study" (Washington, D.C., March 1970).

15. Shea *et al.*, *Years for Decision*, table 6.12.

16. *Ibid.*, table 4.4.

17. *Ibid.*, table 6.8.

18. *Ibid.*, tables 2.9, 5.4.

19. U.S. Department of Labor, *Youth Unemployment and Minimum Wages*, Bulletin 1657 (Washington, D.C.: Government Printing Office, 1970), p. 102.

20. U.S. Department of Labor, Bureau of Labor Statistics, Current Population Survey, "Poverty-Non-Poverty Tracts" (unpublished tabulations, 1970).

The employment problems of black ghetto youth are obviously complex. They are generated by a variety of factors, and though the impact of each may be only marginal at any point in time, they are interdependent and cumulative. These obstacles in aggregate leave the black youth seriously disadvantaged, and he finds it difficult to compete with whites even in the absence of discrimination.

No easy solutions exist to help overcome these obstacles. As with all social problems, there are no panaceas. A systems approach, encompassing a many-faceted attack on the causal factors, is needed. There is a variety of alternative and complementing strategies that could be used or are being used, and all have a role to play. The need for a systems approach, however, does not obviate the necessity of choosing priorities. The entire range of approaches must be examined to determine what each could contribute to solving the problems of nonwhite youths, and those that are most effective should be expanded. The scarce societal resources that will be committed to this end must be allocated as efficiently as possible.

There are several major approaches that have been suggested or used to help solve the employment problems of black youth. Macroeconomic measures are perhaps the most indirect of the strategies, since they affect the whole economy and not just black central city youths. But despite their indirectness they are essential. Through monetary and fiscal policies, the government can regulate aggregate demand which, in turn, affects the level of unemployment. To the degree that nonwhite youths are the "last hired and first fired," they benefit more from reductions in unemployment and suffer more from increases.

Another macroeconomic approach utilizes the minimum wage, which places a floor on wage rates in most industries. Some economists argue that increases in the minimum wage rates over the past decade have had much to do with the rising levels of unemployment among youths. Manipulation or perhaps elimination of the minimum, they say, might reverse the situation, leading to an increased demand for young workers, including many nonwhites. Child labor laws, which regulate the terms and conditions of work by youths, have also had a negative impact on job opportunities for this age group. In some ways their restrictions are anachronistic and could be changed to facilitate the hiring of young workers.

The number of jobs for nonwhite youths can also be increased through microeconomic strategies. Most important are efforts to end discrimination in hiring and upgrading black youths. The major problem for teenagers may be to convince employers that they should experiment with hiring youths no matter what their color. But at the point where nonwhites should move from youth labor markets and employment patterns into more stable and lasting work situations, racial discrimination delays, impedes, or completely prevents the transition. Nonwhites are barred from many occupations and industries, or they are given jobs that have the least potential for improvement. Though such discrimination is illegal it is still widely practiced, and its complete elimination would have a massive impact on opening opportunities to ghetto youths.

Combining carrots with sticks, subsidies can be given for hiring and training disadvantaged nonwhite youths. Ostensibly they can be based on the real costs of employing less productive workers, and there need be no mention of color. But since black youths are more often disadvantaged and since differential costs are difficult to calculate, the subsidy can be used as an incentive to eliminate discriminatory practices. The fact that training is being subsidized means that there is no excuse to turn down the black simply because he is less educated or experienced than the white applicant.

Another approach is to improve the nonwhite youth's preparation for the world of work. While great strides have been made in recent years to reduce school dropout and to increase educational attainment, nonwhites are still far behind whites in their levels of achievement. As long as this is the case, differentials in income and employment levels remain inevitable. Clearly, schooling must be improved through better equipment, better teachers, and a better educational environment.

Remedial training is a related approach. The manpower programs that emerged in the 1960's offer a variety of arrangements for income maintenance, basic and vocational education, health care, counseling, placement, and related assistance. "Training" thus describes a flexible package of services whose purpose is to increase the employability of the participant and his ability to compete for jobs in the private sector.

For many black youths, however, jobs are not available even with training. These youths may need work experience before they can move into gainful employment. Public employment can be used to tide them over until they reach an age when work is easier to find. Other young people may have limited abilities and require a sheltered work situation if they are to work at all.

These strategies have all been tried during the past decade, and their effectiveness can be analyzed at least in part. There are no clear-cut lessons, and assessments of the degree of success or failure may differ widely. But experience yields some indications as to the role the various approaches can play in current efforts.

MANAGING AGGREGATE DEMAND

Black ghetto youths are among the major beneficiaries of a booming economy and are the most frequent victims of its decline. The long-term trend shows that their employment problems have been growing more severe relative to others in the labor force, but cyclical fluctuations around this trend—related to the rise and fall of overall unemployment—have had an even greater impact on their welfare. A comparison of the quarterly changes in average unemployment rates for nonwhite youths in the slum areas of the hundred largest cities with those for white youths throughout these cities demonstrates the impact of cyclical fluctuations (Chart 8).

Between 1967 and 1970, aggregate unemployment declined and then rose precipitously. In the fourth quarter of 1967,

CHART 8. QUARTERLY UNEMPLOYMENT RATES FOR WHITE YOUTHS IN SMSA'S OVER 250,000 AND FOR BLACK YOUTHS IN POVERTY AREAS OF THESE SMSA'S

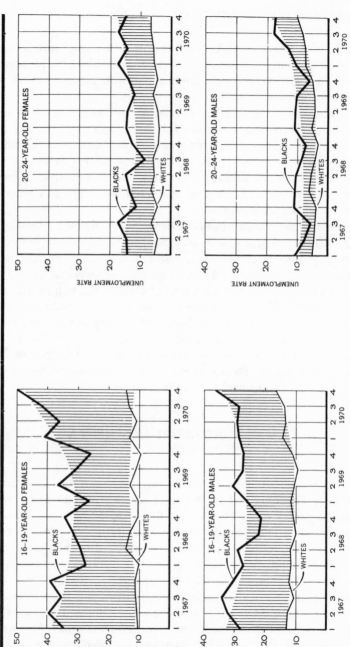

SOURCE: U.S. Department of Labor, Bureau of Labor Statistics, Current Population Survey, "Poverty–Non-Poverty Tracts" (unpublished tabulations, 1970).

unemployment stood at 3.9 percent; by the fourth quarter of 1968, it had fallen to a low of 3.4 percent; but with the subsequent recession it rose to 5.8 percent in the fourth quarter of 1970. Black youths in the ghetto were at the tip of the whiplash of these changes. The 0.5 percentage point drop in aggregate unemployment between the fourth quarter of 1967 and the fourth quarter of 1968 was accompanied by a 9 percentage point decline in the rate, not seasonally adjusted, for black teenage males, a drop of 4 percentage points for black teenage girls, and a smaller but still significant decline for ghetto youths in their early twenties. Conversely, while the aggregate unemployment rate rose 2.4 percentage points between the fourth quarter of 1968 and the fourth quarter of 1970, the rates of black teenagers increased 15 percentage points. Urban white youths are also affected by changes in aggregate conditions, but they are much better off to begin with, and at least young females were not hurt as severely by the economic decline. Whatever the changes in relative unemployment rates, ghetto youths are hardest hit by a slump.

The current alarming increase in unemployment rates for ghetto youths was accompanied by a noticeable decline in their labor force participation. When jobs are scarce, many youths stop looking for work and are not counted among the unemployed. The clearest manifestation of this "discouraged worker" effect is among black females from twenty to twenty-four years old in the ghetto, but it is also evident among black teenagers of both sexes (Chart 9).

The health of the economy is not the only factor causing these dramatic changes. Between 1965 and 1968, the number of potential workers who were drawn out of the civilian labor force by military service increased rapidly; in the last year it declined. This undoubtedly accentuated the changes in unemployment, since fewer workers were available when jobs were plentiful in 1968 but there were more potential workers in 1970 when jobs were scarce. Nevertheless, economic fluctuations undeniably had a significant impact. Females and teenagers were less affected than twenty- to twenty-four-year-old males by the fluctuations in induction levels; yet they had the most pronounced cyclical employment patterns. Nor can the wider fluctuation of unemployment rates among black youths than among whites be explained by the draft alone, because there has been no cyclical pattern in the induction of the two races.

CHART 9. QUARTERLY LABOR FORCE PARTICIPATION RATES FOR WHITE YOUTHS IN SMSA'S OVER 250,000 AND FOR BLACK YOUTHS IN POVERTY AREAS OF THESE SMSA'S

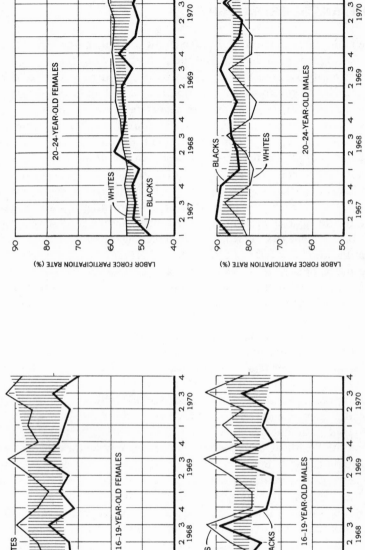

SOURCE: U.S. Department of Labor, Bureau of Labor Statistics, Current Population Survey, "Poverty–Non-Poverty Tracts" (unpublished tabulations, 1970).

The cyclical movements of the economy are therefore the major culprit, with ghetto youth being the major victim of the 1970 slump. Tight labor markets are important for their long-run as well as immediate impact. The strategies aimed at reversing the long-term deterioration of the employment problems of black youth are less effective in a slack economy. Those who participate in training and education problems find their new skills and educational achievements of little value when they have to compete with experienced workers who are out of jobs. Employers are not likely to reexamine or change their hiring practices when employment is down and they can afford to be selective. Improvements in the labor market mechanisms are of little value when the number of unfilled jobs falls dramatically. In other words, efforts to help black youths over the long run will be dissipated in combating the short-run problems resulting from or aggravated by slack economic conditions.

Fiscal and monetary measures geared to stimulate the economy and to increase the aggregate demand for labor are perhaps the most effective way to help black youths. But achievement of full employment is not without costs. A low rate of unemployment can be attained only at the expense of a high level of price increases, while to check prices a higher level of unemployment must be tolerated. Some groups benefit from rising inflation while others are especially hard hit by unemployment. The competing interests must be identified in determining the rates of price increase and unemployment to be sought.

The evidence is persuasive that ghetto youths are best served by lower levels of aggregate unemployment. Few are tied to long-term contracts or commitments, and rising prices are normally compensated by increased earnings. A majority of the low-income families in the ghetto probably benefit from inflation. Some aged poor may be hurt by rising costs, of course, and welfare payments may lag during periods of accelerated inflation. But federal law requires public assistance payments to reflect rises in the cost of living, and the benefits from increasing employment and earnings tend to more than make up for adverse effects. Undeniably, some low-income families will be hurt; however, most will be better off when labor markets are tight.[1]

Few would argue with the need for expansionary economic policies during the slack conditions that occurred throughout 1970.

No one favors an unemployment rate of 6 percent or more, and no one wants 50 percent of the ghetto's teenagers out of work. It is only when aggregate unemployment is reduced, say, to 4 percent that disagreement arises over the efficacy of further expansionary measures. Economists who believe that expansion of demand will have only minimal impact on black employment problems will tend to emphasize "structural" measures, such as public employment and increased training, assuming that the economy cannot absorb all the disadvantaged and that further increases in demand will only lead to inflation. Other economists, who believe that the maintenance of low levels of unemployment will lead to labor market adjustments and the utilization of untapped labor supply, will stress the benefits of still tighter labor markets. The debate between these two camps has abated, but it has not been resolved and is likely to revive as business recovers.

One thing we have learned, however, is that whatever measures are needed to dampen inflation, most ghetto blacks will continue to benefit from expanding demand and declining unemployment. The resulting inflation may be preferable to unemployment that leaves ghetto youth idle on the streets. Structural measures are needed at the same time to employ the hard-core unemployed who have the most severe problems, but an overall unemployment rate around 3.5 percent is a vital goal if progress is to be made in eliminating the causes of severe unemployment among black youth.

THE MINIMUM WAGE AND CHILD LABOR LAWS

Minimum Wages

One factor that may have contributed to the rise of long-term unemployment among nonwhite youths is the minimum wage. Under the Fair Labor Standards Act of 1938, the federal government sets a minimum wage that has to be paid to all workers in specified industries. The scope of the law was expanded during the past decade, raising the proportion of covered workers from 50 percent to 75 percent of all nonsupervisory employees, and the minimum hourly wage rate was raised to $1.60 in 1968. As a result of these increases, the minimum rose from 47.0 percent of the average hourly earnings in private nonfarm employment during 1960 to 55.6 percent in 1968. The increase was even greater relative to the weighted average earnings in industries hiring a large proportion of teenagers.[2]

According to received economic theory, firms faced with increased labor costs because of minimum wage regulations tend to substitute labor-saving machinery for the least productive workers. As profits drop in labor-intensive, low-wage industries, some firms fold and the expansion of others is checked. The overall effect is a reduced demand for low-productivity workers. Since teenagers are usually the most expendable employees and are concentrated in low-wage industries, theory holds that they will bear the brunt of the resulting unemployment.

Despite the impeccable logic of these theoretical arguments, there has been no conclusive proof that youth unemployment has risen as a result of the minimum wage. It is difficult to establish a causal relationship when many other factors are involved. But the evidence that the employment of black youths in particular is significantly reduced by minimum wage legislation cannot be ignored. Not only are they concentrated in low-wage industries where changes in the minimum have their greatest impact; they are also usually the first to be laid off if there are any cutbacks. Each increase in the minimum was accompanied by a rise in the ratio of nonwhite to white unemployment rates for male teenagers. One recent study found that unemployment among nonwhite teenagers increased three times as much as unemployment among white youths with each change in the minimum wage.[3] But an extensive Labor Department analysis showed that minimum wages had no noticeable impact on unemployment of black teenage boys, though they had a definite effect on the labor market status of black teenage girls.[4] To the extent that black youths are bounced out of the minimum wage jobs and forced into the uncovered sector, they are likely to benefit less from the positive income effects than are white youths, while they are more likely to be the victims of resulting unemployment.

More significant, perhaps, is the long-run impact of statutory minimum wages. Over the decades, the increases in the minimum wage may have eliminated jobs that would have remained open to youths. There is no way to measure with any accuracy the magnitude of this impact, but the disturbing long-term increase in the unemployment of black youths warrants consideration of any factors that might have aggravated the problem.

A case can be made for changing minimum wage regulations. But proposals to lower the minimum must be treated as rhetoric. It is unrealistic to expect that Congress will pass legislation to sanction wage cuts. A more acceptable approach is to freeze the statutory minimum for teenagers at present levels as the rates for adult workers rise, as has been recently proposed by the Nixon administration. Although the effects of a dual minimum are not clear-cut,[5] the long-run deterioration of youth employment argues for experimentation.

Child Labor Laws

A reassessment of the child labor laws is also in order. The Fair Labor Standards Act sets a basic minimum working age of sixteen in covered employment, and youths under eighteen are barred from employment in seventeen occupations that are presumed to be hazardous. State laws contain further restrictions. All but five states require an employer to obtain a certificate in order to hire anyone under sixteen, and almost half require work permits for sixteen- and seventeen-year-olds. These restrictions create difficulties or extra costs in hiring youths, and a Labor Department study indicated that child labor regulations have influenced employers not to hire youths before their eighteenth birthday.[6] As a result, young people are not hired in many industries, leaving them to find jobs in the uncovered areas, which are usually less stable and pay less.

The purpose of child labor laws is to prevent the exploitation of young workers. There is no doubt that they accomplish this objective; but they also limit the youngsters' opportunities to work. This limiting effect is rarely considered because of the belief that young people are not capable of protecting their own interests and that in the absence of regulations many employers would take advantage of them.

These assumptions deserve critical examination. Many youths are capable of combining school with work at an early age. They need money to support their life style, and their only alternatives may be illicit activity or idleness. Then too, fewer young people are driven by the stark economic necessity of earlier times. Where exploitation persists, as among migrant workers, it should be controlled, but this is no argument to bar all youngsters from work. Present restrictions are especially inimical to out-of-school youths who are prevented from finding stable and rewarding employment. Experiments are needed to make the laws more flexible and more relevant to current conditions and needs.

EDUCATION FOR EMPLOYMENT

Issues and Answers

The inadequate education of black ghetto youths is a major cause of their labor market problems. But educational improvements are probably not the most effective cure, at least in the short run. The white youth's high school diploma is accepted by employers as a legitimate credential even if it comes from a ghetto school, but it is disregarded if the youth is black. This double standard is based on the employers' perception that the average white is much better educated than the average black with equal years of schooling.

If the quality of the average black student could be improved, it is likely that employers would gradually give more credence to the diploma, though the result would still depend on the extent of discrimination. The issue, however, is whether ghetto schools can be improved and, if so, whether this is the most effective method in terms of cost to ameliorate the employment difficulties of young blacks.

One of the most controversial social issues of our day centers on the means of improving education for disadvantaged youth. Busing, "relevant" curricula, and community control are subjects of angry debate. It is not known whether better facilities will improve learning, whether more qualified teachers can help ghetto youth, whether curricula need to be revised and textbooks rewritten, whether students should be segregated or mixed according to their abilities, whether policemen are needed in schools to keep out rowdies and drug pushers, whether the parents of students should have more say in what is taught, or whether integration to enable children from different socioeconomic groups to rub elbows and share aspirations is a key to helping disadvantaged children.

With so many questions unanswered, it may seem pointless to ask how we can improve education for employment. Certainly the impediments to overall improvement will also be felt in this dimension, but there are reasons to believe that work related instruction can be improved separately and more easily than other aspects of education. The federal government has funded vocational education for over fifty years, and private interests have shown more concern with work preparation than with other facets of education. Because such improvements promise an immediate payoff through increased employability, they will probably be more acceptable to the black community and to youths themselves than other reforms.

Improvement Along Traditional Lines

There is a variety of old and new approaches to improving the preparation for work provided by the school system. The oldest is the vocational education program, the only point of contact that many school curricula have with the world of work. Black youths who enter academic courses generally concentrate on preparation for college—on school for schooling's sake—despite the fact that only a minority will attend. The large proportion in general studies are typically without direction and get little more than a watered-down exposure to academic subjects. Only in vocational education courses are students likely to acquire useful occupational skills and exposure to the demands that will be made outside of school.[7]

The best available estimates indicate that 15 percent of black male students[8] and 18 percent of black female students[9] aged fourteen through seventeen are enrolled in vocational or commercial curricula. The courses can include anything from training in home economics or agriculture to instruction in computer sciences or the latest electronic repair skills. In some schools, vocational education may mean working with outdated equipment, learning through archaic methods, and being taught by teachers who have lost contact with their fields. In other schools, it involves very valuable training that can be translated directly into higher-paying jobs.

Whatever the overall shortcomings of vocational education, many black participants seem to benefit. A number of studies of subsequent labor market experience generally agree that black vocational graduates are better off than those who have pursued other curricula, even though they are more likely to be unemployed and to earn less than white vocational graduates.[10] If more black students can be helped and if the quality of instruction can be improved, the employability of black youth will obviously be enhanced.

Federal legislation in 1963 and 1968 expanded grants to states to finance innovative projects and to facilitate more effective planning. The intent was to expand course offerings in marketable skills. The matching share under programs for the socioeconomically disadvantaged was also increased with the aim of enlarging their enrollment. All these changes, especially the last, could significantly expand the resources available to ghetto schools. To date, however, changes have been slow because vocational educators have been able to resist any undermining of their authority. Help to the "special needs" group still remains meager. In 1969, this group represented only 2 percent of the total vocational education enrollment of more than 7 million.

It is possible to bypass barriers to needed reforms by allocating federal funds directly (or with a mandatory pass-through) to ghetto schools. This approach favors disadvantaged neighborhoods and has been used under the 1965 Elementary and Secondary Education Act and in other antipoverty efforts. There is just as much reason to concentrate vocational education expenditures. With an anticipated growth in resources and enrollments, innovative measures would be easier to introduce than when funding is stable. Whether this effort should precede attempts to improve the total spectrum of education in ghetto schools cannot be known in advance; but judging from the relatively favorable experiences of black vocational education graduates, there is reason to believe that this might be an effective strategy—at least more effective than remedial training measures for dropouts or poor students.

Business and Education

Despair over the difficulties of improving ghetto schools by conventional methods has led to an increasing involvement of business in education. Several large corporations in recent years have offered a wide range of assistance to schools in disadvantaged neighborhoods. Usually they have provided little more than the use of their machinery and some staff time, but others have become involved in cooperative education programs in which the student divides his time between work and school. Some companies have actually provided direct instruction in the school and have promised to employ graduates. General Electric's Corning Lamp Division in Cleveland outfitted and staffed a special school for the disadvantaged, and in Detroit, Chrysler and Michigan Bell "adopted" inner city schools, providing them with equipment, vocational instructors, and other assistance needed to improve the employ-ability of their students, including the development of cooperative programs.[11]

Much has been made of these limited activities, but their effectiveness has not been evaluated carefully and the total number of students who have been helped is meager. Conclusions are necessarily tentative after such limited experience, but the potential contribution of such corporate activities appears minor. There is no reason to expect that employers will be any more willing to involve themselves in education than they have in the federally subsidized training programs, where their voluntary contributions frequently dried up when the publicity value waned. They are even less likely to commit resources and manpower to schools, because this is a more unfamiliar role than hiring and training and because public opinion is extremely sensitive about corporate intrusion into public education.

On the other hand, cooperative education, in which the student's curriculum is adapted to his vocational needs in a particular career, is a promising avenue. This approach requires close coordination between the school and the business community, with each maintaining its traditional role. The constraints here are the resources and manpower needed to provide the necessary individualized attention central to a cooperative program. Increased vocational education funds could be applied for this purpose.

A much more radical approach is "performance contracting," which puts the schools under the control of private firms. Then the output is education itself, and payment to the contractor depends on the measured achievement of students. The contractors, who have control over faculty and teaching methods, therefore have a profit incentive to increase efficiency and to initiate new educational methods.

Through a recent innovation, performance contracting of one sort or another has been tried in more than 200 school districts. The Office of Economic Opportunity has committed $6 million to six companies that will operate school systems in 18 districts. It is still too early to guess whether they will be effective, but some inherent problems can already be detected. For one thing, teachers hardly favor being judged by hard-and-fast rules and being forced to use new methods. It is also likely that the outside firms will become the objects of the varied attacks formerly reserved for school boards and administrators. Another problem is that performance contractors may concentrate on whatever types of knowledge are tested to the exclusion of other instructions. For instance, the General Accounting Office charged that one of the earliest contractors in Texarkana had actually taught pupils the specific questions they would have to answer.[12]

Underlying the support of performance contracting is the promise of getting more education for the dollar. Waste is endemic in the education establishment, and it would be of obvious value to circumvent obstructions to increased efficiency. There is reason to doubt, however, that corporate methods of administration will produce an educational revolution—at least for ghetto blacks. The Job Corps provided a laboratory for some of these techniques, where private firms, including some corporations now involved in performance contracting, ran many of the centers. These activities were not notably successful. Private firms did not show that they were superior to public and nonprofit groups in running Job Corps centers. Perhaps the most successful of the urban centers was operated by the Texas Education Foundation, an independent, nonprofit corporation established by the state of Texas. Its success suggested that given more adequate money, the present educational system could do much better in educating the disadvantaged.[13]

It is unlikely that performance contracting will have a substantial impact on education in the ghetto. There are too many uncertainties and too many uncontrollable factors for businesses to take over ghetto school systems without healthy compensation for the risk. Standards for evaluating performance will be difficult to design and apply since the major purpose of ghetto schools is not to prepare pupils for higher education and since there is already heated debate over the bias of available achievement tests. Past experience does not justify optimism about the potential contributions of performance contracting to ghetto education.

Institutional Change

An even more radical suggestion for improving education is the voucher system, which allows parents and children to choose the public, private, or parochial school they feel provides the best education. Each family is given a voucher equal to the per capita cost of providing public education. The consumers thus have more choice, while the producers have to compete to attract students. This approach in principle allows poor (and nonwhite) children to buy their way into better schools.

Despite its promises, this proposal has many drawbacks. There are measured economies to large-scale public education that alternative systems will not realize. Educational facilities and equipment represent a large investment that should not be wasted by sending children to entirely new institutions. If families are to have freedom of choice for their children's schools, public standards will be difficult to maintain. The ghetto consumer is bilked by all types of merchants, and the appearance of educational merchants is likely if there is a dollar to be made. Those affluent whites who favor segregation will use the vouchers to reduce the cost of attending expensive private schools that are out of reach of the poor. And most significantly, there are very few educational alternatives for ghetto youths. With little income and lacking knowledge about the world outside the ghetto, the vast majority of blacks will almost certainly opt for the schools they now attend.

Another approach is to create new educational institutions, especially those that combine vocational, remedial, and basic education for persons of all ages in the ghetto. One appealing idea is for multipurpose institutions to provide two-year, postsecondary courses, shorter and more specialized vocational instruction, adult basic education and prevocational orientation, perhaps in combination with community college courses. It is a mistake, however, to assume that all the problems of existing institutions can be solved by creating new ones or by combining those already in existence. The money involved in creating new institutions might be spent more effectively in improving the schools that already exist.

The new approaches that some foresee as solutions to ghetto education problems may have favorable results, but they also have many potential shortcomings. They are hardly the panaceas sought by so many people. The more pedestrian route of increasing present educational funds, perhaps with greater emphasis on improving the quality and quantity of vocational instruction in ghetto schools, will probably be more effective than the massive addition of new institutions or drastic changes in administrative or educational methods. At best, it will take a massive inflow of resources and a long time for improvements in ghetto schools to have a major impact on the labor market problems of black youths.

TRAINING AND JOB CREATION

Participation in Federal Manpower Programs

As long as blacks are failing in (or being failed by) the educational system, they will not be able to overcome the economic gap separating them from whites. However, remedial education and training may compensate somewhat for past handicaps. This, at least, is the idea behind the manpower programs initiated in the 1960's to provide compensatory services to the disadvantaged, including a large proportion of black youths. Blacks under twenty-two years of age constitute a major segment of the enrollment, with an estimated 460,000 being served in fiscal 1970 (Table 13).

Because these programs are concentrated in urban areas, ghetto youths are disproportionately represented. In fiscal 1969, there were estimated to be 175,000 sixteen- to twenty-one-year-olds in the

TABLE 13

Major Federally Assisted Manpower Programs and Their Youthful Black Participants

Program Title and Authorizing Legislation	Target Population	Services Provided	Persons Served (thousands)			1970 Estimated Black Enrollment Under 22 Years (thousands)
			1968 actual	1969 actual	1970 estimate	
MDTA Institutional Training Manpower Development and Training Act of 1962, Title II	Mostly unemployed, 16 years of age and over, underutilized workers for upgrading, 2/3 disadvantaged	Occupational training or re-training in a classroom setting at a school or Skill Center; includes testing, counseling, selection, job development, referral and job placement.	140	135	148	50
MDTA On-the-Job Training (OJT) Manpower Development and Training Act of 1962, Title II	Mostly unemployed, preference for 18 year olds and over, 1/2 disadvantaged	Instruction and supervised work at the job site; may include classroom training at vocational education institution or employer's location.	125	130	130	13
Job Corps Economic Opportunity Act of 1964, Title I-A	School dropouts, 16 to 21 years of age, family below poverty level, youth from area with no training opportunities readily accessible	Residential setting with intensive education, skill training, counseling, and related services.	65	53	47	24
Neighborhood Youth Corps (NYC) In-School and Summer	In-school youth, 16 to 21 years of age, family below poverty level	Part time employment and work experience, some counseling.	324	429	445	209
Out-of-School Economic Opportunity Act of 1964, Title I-B	Out-of-school youth, 16 to 18 years of age, family below poverty level	Skill training, remedial education, work experience, counseling, health care.	94	74	37	24

114

Program Title and Authorizing Legislation	Target Population	Services Provided	Persons Served (thousands)			1970 Estimated Black Enrollment Under 22 Years (thousands)
			1968 actual	1969 actual	1970 estimate	
New Careers Economic Opportunity Act of 1964, Title I-B	Disadvantaged adults and out-of-school youths	Work experience and training in human service field; includes basic education, counseling and related services	12	15	20	3
Job Opportunities in the Business Sector (JOBS) Manpower Development and Training Act of 1962 Economic Opportunity Act of 1964	Hard-core unemployed and under-employed, 18 years of age and over, working disadvantaged for upgrading	Orientation, counseling, job related education, minor medical and day care, on-the-job training	107	136	156	70
Concentrated Employment Program (CEP) Manpower Development and Training Act of 1962 Economic Opportunity Act of 1964	Disadvantaged persons in 82 urban poverty and rural deprived areas, predominantly male enrollees	Coordinated delivery of manpower, supportive services	68	140	189	53
Work Incentive Program (WIN) Social Security Amendments of 1967	Recipients of aid to families with dependent children	Training work experience, job creation, basic education, orientation, child care, transportation	—	33	138	14

Source: Bureau of National Affairs, *Manpower Information Service*, Oct. 21, 1970, pp. 21:1006-9; and authors' estimates for final column.

civilian noninstitutional population of the six city slums surveyed by
the Labor Department. Of these, 14,400 had completed manpower
training outside school, the army, or manual apprenticeship
programs. An additional 26,500 were enrolled during the year,
including 16,000 in the Neighborhood Youth Corps.

The manpower programs are a mixed bag, offering different
blends of vocational training, basic education, subsidized employment, income maintenance, and other services. Almost every
program provides a variety of these elements, but the emphasis and
method of delivery differ. For instance, the Manpower Development
and Training Act (MDTA) institutional program and the Job Corps
have stressed training, counseling, and education to increase the
productivity and employability of those who participate. The
Neighborhood Youth Corps, on the other hand, has until recently
stressed work experience in public employment. The Job
Opportunities in the Business Sector (JOBS) program subsidizes the
hiring and training of disadvantaged workers by private employers;
its goal is to persuade firms to lower their hiring standards and to end
their discrimination as well as to provide on-the-job training. While
these programs have much in common, they represent three basically
different approaches: remedial education, creation of jobs in the
public sector, and the subsidizing of employment in the private
sector.

Remedial Education and Training

It is the assumption of the remedial education and training
programs that disadvantaged youth will benefit from a second
chance: improving their reading and arithmetic, orienting them to
the demands of the world of work, and providing them with specific
skills will increase their productivity as workers. This in turn should
lead to lower unemployment, higher wages, and more opportunity
for advancement as employers compete for their skills.

Institutional training was initiated by the MDTA of 1962 to
help workers who had been displaced by technological change.
Gradually, however, it was altered to serve the more disadvantaged,
including black youths. At present 33 percent of its enrollees are

sixteen- to twenty-one-year-old blacks, split evenly between males and females.

The program is aimed at those who are disadvantaged, and who will be able to benefit from training. This dual qualification results in participants who are generally better qualified than enrollees of other manpower programs. The major purpose of the program is to provide vocational training in some skill for which there is a demonstrated demand. For those who are educationally handicapped, however, basic education may be necessary before training is possible. More capable trainees can benefit from the normal courses that usually use public school facilities and their vocational education staffs; but the seriously disadvantaged need the more concentrated assistance offered in special skill centers that combine counseling, education, and other supportive services as well as multioccupational training.

As a rule, black youths benefit less from the program than do other participants. Aggregate institutional data show that black trainees are worse off than whites by almost any measure, while those who are young have especially severe problems and usually find only very low-paying jobs.[14] For example, a follow-up study of youths who participated in programs initiated during 1964 and 1965 found that blacks gained less than whites.[15] During the three- to seven-month period they had been in the labor force since finishing training, 60 percent of white males under the age of twenty had been fully employed, compared with only 33 percent of the blacks, and similar differentials prevailed for black and white girls. The precise estimates are not dependable because of the small sample size, but their message is fairly clear: blacks are less likely than whites to find stable employment even upon successful completion of a training course.

The greater difficulties of blacks cannot be explained by their performance in the program. In fact, a higher proportion of blacks than whites of this age completed training. Yet black youths are willing to participate in training programs because the experience offers them some chance to improve their position. More blacks than whites feel the program offers them a real chance, and many more feel that it is the only alternative even if the benefits will be limited because of the inequities in the marketplace.

In contrast to the MDTA-institutional program, the Job Corps concentrates on a much more disadvantaged clientele. It was initiated by the Economic Opportunity Act of 1964 with the express purpose of helping those who are most disadvantaged. By removing youths aged from sixteen to twenty-one from their debilitating home environments and placing them in residential centers where they would combine useful work with intensive basic education, skill training, counseling, and other services, it was hoped that they could be saved from a future of dependency and offered a second chance in life.

To this end, the enrollees have come from the most extremely disadvantaged group. In 1970, almost 66 percent were black—61 percent male and 39 percent female. Among the blacks, only 4 percent of the boys and 25 percent of the girls had completed high school.

Working intensively with such a disadvantaged group while providing them with room and board, the Job Corps is understandably expensive. Annual costs are still around $6,500 per enrollee despite drastic cost-cutting since the program was initiated in 1965. Unfortunately, the results to date have not demonstrated that the investment is justified. For one thing, new methods of education have not proved as effective as many had hoped. The enrollees who had trouble their first time through school have almost as much difficulty the second time around. The most valid conclusion seems to be that Job Corps educational gains are probably not greater than those of public schools, though they are probably better than the rates the same individuals maintained in public school. The vocational training may be more useful. Obviously the value of skill training depends on its intensity, and those who stay longer in the Job Corps are more likely to use their skills.

The real issue, however, is whether Job Corps men and women improve their earnings and employment status as a result of their participation in the program. Follow-up studies suggest that the gains in earnings of former enrollees (white and black) were slight in comparison with a control group and that the incidence of unemployment among the blacks was not noticeably affected by the Job Corps experience.

Several conclusions can be drawn from the experience of the MDTA-institutional and Job Corps programs. First, black youths are likely to benefit less from training than whites whether or not they successfully complete their programs, again indicating that blacks do not have an equal chance to compete with whites when they return to the labor market. Second, remedial programs for the severely disadvantaged youths from the ghetto are expensive while the improvements in employability are not likely to be impressive. And third, blacks who can be trained without prior remedial education will usually find the programs a stepping stone to better jobs even though training is of less benefit to them than it is to whites. Since there are so many blacks with fair academic records and abilities who nevertheless earn little and are victims of underemployment, it might be better to concentrate manpower resources on providing specific skills that will facilitate entry into better paying jobs—for instance, typing and shorthand for female black high school graduates. Public employment or subsidized private employment may be needed for the hard-core unemployed who gain little from institutional training.

Employment in the Public Sector

The most direct way to help black youths who cannot find jobs is to put them to work in the public sector. Ideally, training can be provided along with work experience so that participants will be able to compete for jobs in the marketplace. A youth employment program would thus help youths through their most difficult years while enhancing their employability. In the process they would be kept off the streets and, we hope, out of trouble.

This was the concept behind the Neighborhood Youth Corps (NYC) initiated under the Economic Opportunity Act of 1964 in response to growing concern with the problems of disadvantaged youths. An in-school segment provides part-time work and income to students in the hope that this assistance will help reduce the number who leave school for economic reasons. But the out-of-school and summer programs are more characteristically public employment efforts.

Out-of-school NYC provides work for sixteen- and seventeen-year-old dropouts who come from poor families. Most of the jobs are in the public or nonprofit sector, at entry-level work requiring few skills, and antipoverty community action agencies are the major sponsors. Men are usually assigned to maintenance and custodial work, while women typically work in clerical or health positions. Most of these jobs pay near the minimum wage, with extra stipends for household heads with dependents.

The out-of-school NYC program has had a checkered career. It was initiated with high hopes and reached an average enrollment of 99,000 in fiscal 1966. The shortcomings of the program were increasingly recognized, however, leading to a drastic cut in average enrollment to 45,000 in fiscal 1970. The major failing was that project sponsors made few efforts to utilize the skills of participants fully, because they were free labor and there was no price attached to inefficiency. Stripped of their titles, almost all the jobs were menial and unattractive, and little basic education was provided to improve the employability of the participants.

The inadequacy of the services and the irrelevance of the work experience provided by out-of-school NYC were reflected in the small number of participants who moved on to private sector jobs, even in the tight labor markets of 1967 and 1968. A comprehensive follow-up of enrollees leaving the program between January and September 1966 showed that forty weeks after termination, less than 40 percent were employed, more than 25 percent were not in the labor force or school, and 12.6 percent were looking for jobs but unable to find them.[16] Thus, nearly 25 percent of those who were in the labor force were unemployed, a proportion about equal to that of comparable youths who were not enrolled in NYC.

The current plans are to revamp the program and increase budgeted annual expenditures per enrollee from $3,000 to $3,700 to provide more intensive vocational training and education. The experience, however, has taught painful lessons that must be kept in mind when considering increased public employment efforts. For one thing, it is difficult to create meaningful jobs for youthful participants. Despite the claims of unmet manpower needs in the urban areas, few cities have been able to place young dropouts in productive work, for even the most menial jobs require some training and skill. While entry-level jobs are available in many areas, it is difficult to use large numbers of NYC enrollees unless they are assigned on a full-time basis and are funded from regular payrolls. Temporary public employment for out-of-school youth almost unavoidably means dead end, unattractive jobs at low wages with few opportunities for advancement.

A second lesson is that public employment during the teen years will not significantly improve the chances of later employment. Training and basic education may increase employment opportunities, but employment itself does not lead to increased employability. The program can even have negative effects when a sheltered and attractive work environment is created that is less demanding than work in the private sector.

A final lesson is that public employment may be ineffective for all but the most severely handicapped males. Even when unemployment rates are high, few are attracted to jobs in the public sector that carry the stigma of failure and pay extremely low wages. Life on the street is more alluring, and some other work can often be found.

On the positive side, public employment can be very important to females who have no other options. The experience has been that female applicants are more numerous than males, that they are far less likely to drop out once they get in, and that the jobs that can be provided for them are more attractive and productive. Except for determined attempts to maintain a balanced sexual distribution in out-of-school NYC projects, the females would have far outnumbered males. The redistribution of slots among boys and girls should be considered in light of the very serious employment problems of black girls in urban areas. Public employment of the NYC variety could open opportunities that are available nowhere else.[17]

The summer segment of NYC has a different focus, but its experience also contains important lessons about public employment programs for youths. Its aim is to provide income and part-time work during the summer for sixteen- to twenty-one-year-old students from poor families. The purposes of the program are much narrower than those of out-of-school NYC: there is little emphasis on enrichment or meaningful work experience. The projects are sponsored by public or nonprofit agencies and usually hire youths for twenty-six hours per week for ten weeks at a rate of $1.45 per hour.

Appropriations permitting, the enrollment in summer NYC grows larger each year. About 400,000 slots were funded in the summer of 1970 and about 50 percent more were provided the subsequent year. It is estimated that about 50 percent of the enrollees are black, there being a slightly higher percentage of males than females, and most of these are inner city youths. The program is viewed by many as antiriot insurance, and each year as summer approaches cities panic and ask for increased funding. Congress invariably delays action until the middle of the summer and thus precludes any project planning. In 1970, Congress appropriated supplementary funds for summer NYC in July when only seven weeks remained to fill the slots and to spend the money, and it did only slightly better in 1971.

The summer NYC experiences demonstrate that the number of youths who can be put to work in the warm summer months on a part-time basis is many times greater than NYC enrollments. Every city has applicants who have to be turned away owing to lack of funds. There are countless teenagers who want to work, even in menial tasks at $1.45 an hour, but cannot find jobs. Summer NYC partially fills this need and does keep a larger number of otherwise idle youths occupied.

The program also suggests that in creating short-duration make-work positions, it may be easier to employ males than females. Despite the fact that summer employment problems are much more severe for black girls than for boys, the NYC mix favors the latter. This is a matter of policy in many localities, but it also reflects the fact that outdoor physical work slots are usually the most easily created on short notice.

Expanded public employment efforts have been suggested as a remedy for the growing youth unemployment in the ghetto. There can be no doubt that summer and out-of-school NYC can and should be expanded with the declining demand in the private sector, but it is not likely to fill all the needs. The number of unemployed sixteen- to nineteen-year-old nonwhites in the SMSA's with a population over 250,000 rose from 41,000 in early 1969 to 75,000 by the end of the following year. In addition, perhaps 10,000 more dropped out of the labor force because they could not find jobs. Just to employ the black sixteen- to nineteen-year-olds major SMSA's who have been forced into idleness by the economic decline would cost an estimated $163 million, assuming the average annual cost of $3,700 per out-of-school NYC enrollee. To employ all the black sixteen- to nineteen-year-olds in these large urban areas who were out of work in January 1971 would require nearly $300 million. The additional cost of helping disadvantaged white teenagers, blacks in smaller cities, and the twenty- to twenty-four-year-olds who could not find jobs might involve a multibillion dollar price tag.

The high cost is not the only drawback. Public employment apparently yields meager benefits to youthful participants. There is little evidence that the jobs and training provided under summer and out-of-school NYC contribute perceptibly to increasing the employability of participants. The work is rarely productive, and the youths gain few skills that can help them in the private sector. Unless substantial changes are made in NYC, its goals must remain modest—to keep youths off the street until opportunities or responsibilities increase with age.

Despite these shortcomings, public employment is the only proven way to help ghetto youths when labor markets are slack. Even if it provides no training and accomplishes little useful work, public employment may be justified in a recession. With improvements that are possible, it might also serve as an important means of assisting the most disadvantaged youth who need help even in the best of times.

Subsidies to Private Employers

The overwhelming majority of ghetto youths must depend on jobs in the private sector where approximately 85 percent of employed black youths now work. Doubling of government employment will still leave 70 percent dependent on private sector jobs. For this reason, partnership programs to hire and train disadvantaged youths, combining government subsidies and other assistance with private efforts by businessmen, are of primary importance.

The largest partnership program is Job Opportunities in the Business Sector (JOBS). Initiated in 1968, JOBS offers federal subsidies to private employers who agree to hire and train specifically designated disadvantaged workers. But the heart of the program is the voluntary participation by the private sector. The National Alliance of Businessmen (NAB)—initially staffed primarily by executives on leave from large corporations—has administrative responsibility over the program. More significantly, a number of firms have agreed to hire and train disadvantaged workers without subsidy.

The target population of the JOBS program, the disadvantaged worker, is defined to include the poor who are school dropouts, persons under twenty-two or over forty-five years of age, and members of minority groups. The Labor Department estimated that in fiscal 1970 nearly 50 percent of the contract hires were less than twenty-two years old and that most of the youths were black males. This makes the JOBS program the single most important manpower effort for black youth other than NYC.

Unfortunately, JOBS was hurt by the economic slump of 1970. An increasing proportion of hires have been subsidized rather than voluntary, and it has not been easy to find takers for these subsidies despite loosened requirements and stepped-up efforts to sell the program. This experience suggests that private sector programs are not very effective in a slack economy. "Corporate consciousness" is apparently a boom-time luxury, and even federal subsidies lose their attractiveness when qualified workers are actively seeking jobs. It would be a mistake, however, to blame the economic decline for other shortcomings in the JOBS program, just as it would be a mistake to assume that the approach can be automatically expanded when prosperity returns.

For one thing, reported hiring figures were more than generous in counting voluntary placements. Even where the hires were real and disadvantaged persons were employed, they were often those who would have gotten the jobs without the program. Little is known about the training offered under JOBS, but according to evidence gathered by the General Accounting Office in five cities, it is frequently little more than what is normally offered. The $2,800 average subsidies under contract were apparently more for hiring than for training, since janitors, common laborers, and office boys were included among the filled positions. The GAO concluded that most of the contract jobs were low-skill and vulnerable to technological change and that a training program might have been more helpful to those workers hired under JOBS.[18]

Whatever success the JOBS program may have had in the past, two major factors constrain further expansion when prosperity returns. First, voluntary participation by employers has had very definite limitations, and hires cannot be expanded simply by increasing appeals to corporate conscience. One of the major reasons businesses participated in JOBS was the publicity value. As more firms hire disadvantaged workers and advertise their commitment, the value diminishes. It is likely that the limits of such superficial commitment have already been reached, and the scale of voluntary efforts attained in late 1968 and early 1969 will be difficult to repeat.

Second, if voluntary efforts will not expand, subsidies will clearly have to be increased to enlarge the scale of the program. The firms that can most effectively hire and train disadvantaged workers will be the first to participate and will demand only modest subsidies. To attract a firm with little use for such efforts, greater incentives will be needed. There is very definitely a limit to the proportion of disadvantaged that any company can afford and is willing to employ.

Despite these shortcomings and constraints, the JOBS program has been a significant help to young blacks, giving them jobs and income as well as work experience. Even considering that many who were hired would have found similar employment, the number of youths who benefited was probably greater than that under any other manpower program except NYC. Though the JOBS approach may be useful only when employers are driven by labor shortages to accept black applicants, it can be effective then. If unemployment can be reduced, intensified antidiscrimination measures could stimulate the demand for black workers and employers might turn to JOBS to help them comply with equal opportunity requirements. This would be a most warranted use of federal subsidies.

It is imperative, however, that voluntarism be rekindled if the program is to be expanded. More than ever before, public and priate pressure must be brought to bear on corporation executives to convince them that voluntary abandonment of discrimination is necessary for their own good. Better administrative procedures must also be instituted to ensure that the government and the individuals hired receive a fair return for the subsidies. The government must develop criteria to assure the hiring of persons who would not have got jobs without the subsidies and the relation of government outlays to real training costs.[19]

If these changes can be made, employer subsidies can be an effective way of getting more black youths out of the secondary labor market and into the mainstream economy. The JOBS program's primary focus should continue to be this clientele and should emphasize providing permanent job opportunities.[20]

COMBATING DISCRIMINATION

Limited Efforts

There can be little argument that discrimination is widespread, affecting all aspects of blacks' employment experience. On the whole, they are hired last, fired first, paid the least, and given the most unattractive jobs. Blacks of all ages are set back by these practices, but youths are hurt perhaps even more than others. They have difficulty in finding even low-paying jobs, but most of all they are denied access to the occupations, the industries, and the tracks within each firm that promise a better future. Even more serious than the high rates of unemployment experienced in the teens is the inability of ghetto youths in their early twenties to match the favorable occupational and industry shifts that are made by white youths. The discrimination that channels black youths into the secondary labor market is at least as detrimental as that which restricts the number of jobs.

The nation's record of fighting discrimination has not been impressive. There have been many federal efforts, but they have been meagerly supported and have had little impact.[21] The Equal Employment Opportunities Commission (EEOC), created by the Civil Rights Act of 1964, has the broadest scope but the feeblest tools. Under current law the five-man commission may investigate a complaint of discrimination, and if it finds the complaint just, it may attempt a voluntary conciliation between the employer and the employee. It has no enforcement powers, and if conciliation fails the employee must take the employer to court on his own initiative and bear the substantial costs. Through 1970 the commission had received roughly 45,000 charges, more than half involving racial discrimination, but it was able to conciliate less than 9,000. This record hardly makes a dent in the problem of discrimination.

The dismal performance of the EEOC can be attributed to the lack of funding and the lack of enforcement powers. Despite the expansion of appropriations from $3 million in fiscal 1966 to a budgeted $19 million for fiscal 1971 and the growth of personnel to 1,165 full-time employees, manpower and resources remain totally inadequate.

More power is also needed, since employers can usually ignore the EEOC's efforts with little fear of reprisal. Proposed legislation would extend coverage to state and local government employees, would give the commission the authority to issue cease-and-desist orders to enforce its findings of discrimination, and would empower it to bring action in the courts against any violators. This would certainly put EEOC in a better position to demand compliance with its decisions and would lift the burden of litigation from the aggrieved.

Another agency charged with combating discrimination is the Office of Federal Contract Compliance (OFCC), which has the authority to delay or cancel any federal contracts with employers who do not take "affirmative action" toward equal employment. Those who are especially recalcitrant can be denied government contracts. If enforced, this power would have far-reaching significance. Defense Department contracts extend to all levels of industry; the General Services Administration buys from a vast array of suppliers in its procurement and construction operations; the Post Office Department has contracts with transportation and communication industries as well as builders; and the Departments of Health, Education, and Welfare and Housing and Urban Development also have broad market influences. Each of these departments and many other agencies have their own contract compliance personnel to police equal opportunity activities, and they report to the staff of the OFCC.

Executive Order 11246, which gives the OFCC its broad powers, is more inclusive in combating discrimination than the Civil Rights Act. The order not only precludes discrimination but requires contractors to take positive steps to overcome its effects. In some instances, especially areawide bargaining with builders, this has been interpreted to mean that equal entry is not sufficient but that quotas or manning tables can be required to bring minority participation up to stated levels.

In reality, however, contractors frequently ignore or postpone contract compliance recommendations because the OFCC is reluctant to use its powers. Sanctions have been rare, with only a few contracts delayed or given to equal opportunity employers rather than to blacklisted low bidders. Overall implementation of Executive Order 11246 has been decidedly cautious despite the publicity given to the Philadelphia and other plans to force construction contractors to hire blacks. There are other tools available to the federal government for fighting discrimination. All grants-in-aid to states contain a prohibition against discrimination in employment. Since federally supported programs are vital to states and localities, the antidiscrimination provisions could have a major impact if enforced. The Federal Civil Service could also take more vigorous steps to reduce discrimination within the federal government.

The Case of the Construction Industry

These antidiscrimination efforts have had little impact on youths generally. The problems of teenage workers have gone all but unnoticed, and though workers in their early twenties have been helped somewhat, most emphasis has been directed to combating discrimination in skilled occupations that involve mostly adult workers. A notable exception has been the effort to eliminate entry barriers to blacks, especially youths, in the construction trades. This example demonstrates both the difficulties and potentialities of helping those just entering the world of work.

The construction industry offers many attractive job opportunities, especially for unionized workers. Entry into the skilled trades is largely controlled by the unions, which also play a dominant role in apprenticeship programs. Because of traditional exclusion from these programs, blacks are underrepresented in the higher-paying constructions jobs. While they constituted 30.5 percent of unionized laborers, 14.0 percent of plasterers and 13.5 percent of the roofers in 1967, they accounted for only 0.6 percent of unionized electrical workers, 1.6 percent of carpenters, 3.7 percent of painters, and 0.2 percent of sheet metal workers.[22]

Racial discrimination is not the only reason for this underrepresentation of blacks in the skilled trades. They are less aware of opportunities, and because few of their friends or relatives are in the trades black youngsters rarely aspire to train in these highly skilled occupations. Because of earlier handicaps, few are willing or able to meet the rather strict entry requirements. Nevertheless, racial discrimination is both overt and covert. The apprenticeship system itself, with its subjective entry standards, its reliance on passing skills from father to son, and its exclusionary purpose, is inherently discriminatory. Blacks fully as able as whites have fewer opportunities even if they do find out about and apply for apprenticeship slots.

Some progress has been made over the past decade in correcting this situation. Many factors have been involved, and the experience is instructive. First, blacks have continually pressured the unions, employers, and governments through repeated demonstrations, demanding quotas in many cities and halting work on public construction. Second, the AFL-CIO leadership and its Building Trades Council have spoken out against discrimination and have aided efforts to get blacks into the trades. Third, the federal government has used its market power to demand hiring quotas or at least positive steps toward the elimination of discrimination. Some city governments, such as that of Chicago, have bent to local pressure by earmarking a stated number of jobs for blacks in public construction. Fourth, federally and privately sponsored outreach programs have been initiated to convince blacks to apply and to help them train for positions that have been inaccessible to them in the past. And finally, many local unions operating in central cities voluntarily abandoned their discriminatory practices. Though local union leaders may have resented the threats of black militants, they could not ignore these blacks' power to halt or hinder construction.

The progress in opening apprenticeships can be considered significant only in light of the previously almost complete exclusion of blacks. It has had an inconsequential impact on the overall problems of nonwhite youths, affecting only a small number of males who are mostly high school graduates. The experience does suggest, however, that even the most entrenched discriminatory practices can be overcome when public pressure, minority group activism, governmental policy, and upper-echelon private leadership combine to carry out a social goal.

The Potential of Government Action

The government's antidiscrimination measures must take the ·lead in this effort. Its market and legal powers are potent tools to combat entrenched cases of discrimination. Federal officials must also assume the responsibility for pinpointing the problem areas and coordinating private sector efforts. But to play this more active role, they will need more money, more manpower, more authority, and, above all, a greater commitment to the goal. The EEOC can become an effective agency if it is granted cease-and-desist powers and the resources to utilize them fully. The OFCC can have a massive impact if the president's mandate is translated into administrative pressure. Federal grant programs can be an instrument of change at the state and local level, if funds are more strictly tied to compliance with equal opportunity guidelines. If discrimination is to be reduced, there is no alternative to leadership by the government.

The difficult questions are where, how, and for whom these efforts should be directed. For instance, the EEOC can choose among a variety of procedures. It may react to complaints filed by individuals, in which case its efforts may have little carry-over effect. It may single out industries that demonstrate recognizable patterns of discrimination and concentrate efforts by pursuing cases with broad repercussions.

Attacking discrimination on an aggregate basis, for instance through quota systems, requires the availability of black workers with the requisite skills. It would be unrealistic to demand that firms fill a predetermined proportion of technical jobs with nonwhites if a sufficient number of adequately trained applicants were not available. This would make firms bear the burden of compensating for the inadequacies nonwhites might have because of past experiences and for which the firms may share little responsibility. It also does little for the dignity of blacks to accept jobs for which they are not qualified. On the other hand, positive steps must be taken to ensure that blacks are being prepared for and provided equal access to better jobs.

As long as funds and manpower are in short supply, a choice must also be made between helping men or women, older or younger workers, and those who are skilled or unskilled. These choices are disguised where action is based on individual complaints, but they are implicit since only a minority of cases can be pursued.

There are several arguments for increasing the emphasis on helping nonwhite youths. Where blacks are shunted into a separate track that promises little chance for the future, the elimination of discrimination at an early juncture may allow them to follow the same route as whites. Where the two paths diverge increasingly, an early effort may be the only expedient. It may also be easier to recognize and overcome discrimination at an early stage, before the more limited training and advancement opportunities of blacks have left them too far behind whites. Another consideration is that the approach of attacking a pattern of discrimination may be more effective because young workers just starting out have few skills and are, for the most part, involved in entry-level jobs. These arguments are intensified by the fact that nonwhite youth employment problems are growing worse while those of older blacks show long-term improvement. For this, if for no other reason, more attention should be given to eliminating discrimination in youth labor markets.

WE CAN DO MORE!

The only sure way to eliminate the employment problems of ghetto youth is to increase the scale of efforts massively on all fronts. More money can be spent for schools, family support, remedial training, birth control programs, public employment, placement and counseling, ghetto economic development, private hiring and training, fighting discrimination, and myriad other efforts affecting the lives of black youths. Improvements unquestionably are needed in many areas, and efforts in all these directions have a valid claim for funds and other recources.

It is a fact of life, however, that resources are and will continue to be limited. It is the difficult task of policymakers to choose among alternative approaches, allocating their scarce resources and efforts where they will do the most good. Rational allocation of resources requires knowledge about the comparative cost and effectiveness of alternative measures. Such knowledge can never be unequivocal, and it is likely to be highly controversial. Nevertheless, careful analysis can provide at least some general guidelines for public policy.

If the preceding arguments are valid, the most effective strategy to improve the employment problems of black youths would have five major elements. First, monetary and fiscal policies would be applied to achieve an unemployment rate of 3.5 percent, which is probably the best single solution to existing difficulties. Second, measures to combat discrimination would be strengthened and implemented more vigorously, placing emphasis on the employment problems of black youths. Third, resources would be provided to alleviate the plight of young black women, providing some alternative to dependency through subsidies to private employers or through expanded public employment. Fourth, greater effort would be directed to increasing the demand for young workers, including experimentation with a dual minimum wage and revision of child labor laws. And, fifth, public employment programs would be expanded as a stopgap measure, with an understanding that services would be intensified and extended to the most disadvantaged youths when conditions improve.

This strategy would stop short of a concerted attack on the difficulties of black youth. Their rates of unemployment will continue to be higher than those of whites, their wage rates lower, and their chances of getting the more rewarding jobs slimmer as long as they are being raised in low-income, unstable homes, are going to inferior schools, and are living in an atmosphere of crime and squalor. Unless all of these conditions are improved, their employment problems will be more severe than those of white youths.

If a massive effort could be mounted and more resources allocated to combat all the interrelated deficiencies of ghetto life, a much different strategy would be needed. A full-scale attack on these problems would have to move on several fronts at once: funds for central city education might be expanded severalfold; locational subsidies might be provided to help black families move to the suburbs; urban renewal efforts might bulldoze parts of the city to provide better housing for blacks; crime control might be dramatically increased, with improvements in the rehabilitation of youthful offenders; and income subsidies might be provided to all, but with strong incentives to reward those who work. These measures would be extremely costly, and their acceptability is questionable in the present political climate. If more people realized the seriousness of ghetto problems and the dire consequences of current trends, they might recognize that massive and extreme efforts are needed.

These policy measures can ameliorate the currently deplorable conditions in the ghetto and give black youths a better chance than they have now. It is doubtful that they can check the tide of deterioration in the central cities, but they may be able to hold the line until we are able to make progress against the deeper causes of urban deterioration. Alleviating the employment problems of young blacks is as good a starting point as any, and the need for immediate action is obvious to all who open their eyes. There are no proven measures and no paths to guaranteed success. But action should not be delayed by a continuing debate over the most effective means. The outlined strategies are likely to result in a high immediate payoff at acceptable costs. Other long-run and more costly strategies may be preferred, and if the needed resources can be committed, they will have a more lasting impact.

NOTES

1. Robinson H. Hollister and John L. Palmer, "The Impact of Inflation on the Poor" (Discussion Paper No. 40-69, Institute for Research on Poverty, University of Wisconsin, 1969).

2. U.S. Department of Labor, *Youth Unemployment and Minimum Wages*, Bulletin 1657 (Washington, D.C.: Government Printing Office, 1970), p. 12.

3. Gene Chapin and Douglas Adie, "Teenage Unemployment Effects of Federal Minimum Wages," paper presented at the 22d annual meeting of the Industrial Relations Research Association, Detroit, Mich., December 28, 1970, p. 8.

4. U.S. Department of Labor, *Youth Unemployment*, p. 38.

5. *Ibid.*, pp. 107-34.

6. *Ibid.*, pp. 90-94.

7. Rupert Evans, "School for Schooling's Sake," in *The Transition From School to Work* (Princeton, N.J.: Princeton University, 1968).

8. Herbert Parnes *et al.*, *Career Thresholds*, vol. 1, Manpower Research Monograph no. 16, Manpower Administration, U.S. Department of Labor (Washington, D.C.: Government Printing Office, 1970), p. 26.

9. John Shea *et al.*, *Years for Decision*, vol. 1 (Columbus, Ohio: Center for Human Resource Research, The Ohio State University, 1971), p. 5.

10. Jeffrey Piker, *Entry into the Labor Force: A Survey of Literature on the Experience of Negro and White Youths* (Ann Arbor: Institute of Labor and Industrial Relations, University of Michigan, 1968), pp. 54-60.

11. "Industry—New Partner in Education," *Scholastic Teacher*, March 21, 1969, pp. 10-15.

12. "The Customers Pass the Test—or Else," *Business Week*, September 12, 1970, p. 42.

13. Sar A. Levitan, *The Great Society's Poor Law* (Baltimore: The Johns Hopkins Press, 1969), p. 280.

14. Sar A. Levitan and Garth L. Mangum, *Federal Training and Work Programs in the Sixties* (Ann Arbor: Institute of Labor and Industrial Relations, University of Michigan, 1967), part 2.

15. Gerald Gurin, *A National Attitude Study of Trainees in MDTA Institutional Programs* (Ann Arbor: Institute for Social Research, University of Michigan, 1970), table 51.

16. Dunlap and Associates, *Survey of Terminees From Out-of-School Neighborhood Youth Corps Projects* (Darien, Conn: Dunlap and Associates, May 1967).

17. Edwin Harwood, "A Tale of Two Cities," *The Public Interest*, fall 1969, pp. 78-87.

18. U.S. General Accounting Office, "Evaluation of Program Results and Administration of the Job Opportunities in the Business Sector (JOBS) Program" (February 1970; mimeographed).

19. Jules Cohn, *The Conscience of the Corporations* (Baltimore, Md.: The Johns Hopkins Press, 1971).

20. Charles Myers, "Hiring and Training the Disadvantaged," in *The Role of the Private Sector in Manpower Development* (Baltimore, Md.: The Johns Hopkins Press, 1971), pp. 24-51.

21. Richard P. Nathan, *Jobs and Civil Rights* (Washington, D.C.: Government Printing Office, 1969).

22. Vernon M. Briggs, "Black Entry Into the Apprenticeship Trade: Lessons of the Sixties and Prospects for the Seventies," paper delivered at the Indiana University Manpower Conference, March 20, 1970 (mimeographed), p. 4.